# CREDIT REPAIR TACTICAL GUIDE

## DISCOVER SECRETS ON HOW TO DISPUTE WITH CREDIT BUREAUS, SETTLE DEBTS, AND PREPARE FOR BANKRUPTCY

J. C. ALLEN

# CONTENTS

# HOW TO GET THE MOST OUT OF THIS BOOK

If you're genuinely curious, willing to make changes, and take action, you can be on your way towards a debt-free future. To help you on your journey, I have created a free workbook that includes an easy to use budgeting sheet & debt calculator to determine your debt-free date. Use this tool to guide you in accomplishing your goals.

To get the most out of this book, sign up now by visiting the link below:

https://allenanything.com

SCAN ME

# FOREWORD

Your credit will thank you for reading this book!

I believe everyone wants an excellent credit score, but only a few are really committed to working for it. After all, good credit is not bought; it's earned. I remember being in a place of complete financial knowledge deficit. My father was diagnosed with a brain tumor. Due to the medication he was prescribed, he had complications, which led him to be in the hospital for nearly four months. Getting let go from my job at Chase bank for not attending to my post since my father was living day by day, my financial struggles began. Two cars repossessed, living by using our credit cards and getting them charged off, and eventually ending in collections. Before I knew it, we were in debt of nearly $113 thousand. Bankruptcy seemed like the "way to go," and my wife and I filed with little to no information. Needless to say, life after bankruptcy gets much more challenging after that (from a pride and financial standpoint!). After coming from filing bankruptcy myself, learning about how to restore my credit back to health, and helping thousands of people do the same, I feel like J.C. Allen is taking me to school with this new book! The way he puts you in the lender's shoes to determine credit worthiness gives you a different perspective of credit that most don't consider. Most of us are emotionally attached to our borrowing power, yet Allen gives you a logical approach to understanding this!

Take it coming from someone who looks at credit reports every day for a living; It's not enough to just "want" great credit. You need to learn to understand it; otherwise, you will be spinning around in the same circle and end with the same results. Allen understands this and explains it from the beginning, teaching you how the credit bureaus work and make money using your data (our credit report is the bread and butter of bureaus) to different financial options you have for improving your finances and credit.

Allen does not sugarcoat the reality of bad credit. From talking about the lack of financial knowledge in our school system to the fact that there is no fast and easy way to fix bad credit. Most credit books will tell you, "this is your credit bible, and you do not need anything else." Yet Allen talks about tools that you can actually use to help yourself to understand credit better.

One significant thing J.C. Allen talks about is the "Illusion of bankruptcy." I was under the impression that bankruptcy would be the answer to my problems.

Through my daily consultations with different clients, I see a repetitive pattern in certain people. Those who don't learn from their previous failures will always be chasing the opportunity to a fresh start, as Allen puts it. This book gives you perspective and insight one would never think of since our focus is usually locked in on one thing, to get good credit! But it is not enough to get good credit; you need to learn to eliminate the root of the problem! Allen describes the different services and their individual focus throughout the book so you as a consumer can make a decision that makes financial sense to you! Most books out there on the market focus on one thing but not this book! Read to learn the options you have at your fingertips!

As I recall, when my wife and I filed for bankruptcy after taking mandatory credit counseling, we were not ahead of the place we had originally started. Our financial literacy and inability to handle our paycheck were exactly at the same level as before our bankruptcy. Reading this book will put you in a different headspace for a few reasons:

1. You are presented with different options as a consumer and
2. The very fact that you are reading the book shows that you are committed to taking a different approach to how you are trying to handle your finances.

One of the most important things to remember about the content of this book is that every single choice you make will affect your credit differently. This tactical guide will illustrate what each option would look like, keep in mind that every credit file is different.

If you are truly serious about your credit being repaired and you do not want to pay, you need to learn how to communicate with credit bureaus, creditors, debt collectors, and look into negotiating your debts when necessary. Allen gives you five steps to credit repair, but my personal favorite is step 5! Not only does he focus on showing you insights to repairing your credit, but also on rebuilding it! Something most people forget about!

You and I have something In common, finances will affect us for the rest of our lives. Positive or negative, that is an individual choice. After reading this book, you will not have an excuse to fail at making better financial decisions.

-Ricardo Soto

The Financial ER

# INTRODUCTION

A low credit score can severely limit your ability to live a life of financial freedom. Your credit score determines the interest rates on any loans you take out, what kinds of credit cards you're eligible for, whether or not you get approved to rent particular apartments, and sometimes even what types of jobs you can get. In short, it's crucial to maintain a healthy credit score because a poor one can sabotage you in a variety of different ways.

Despite their best intentions, many people struggle to reach and keep the type of credit score that qualifies them for the best loan rates and other benefits. If you find that your score is far lower than what you would like it to be, you're not alone. Maybe you had a financial emergency that drained your bank account and left you in so much debt you couldn't hope to pay it off before it damaged your score. Maybe you got in over your head with your spending habits and consistently missed payments on your credit card bills. Perhaps you never learned the best methods for managing your money, so you struggled with fiscal responsibility because you didn't have the tools you needed to succeed. Whatever the case may be, bad credit is like a shadow that clings to you and holds you back, and it's essential to ditch this shadow as soon as possible so you can enjoy the upsides of having excellent credit.

No matter how low your score is currently, you can raise it if you know how. One thing is for sure: you're not going to improve your score if you continue practicing bad spending habits that got you into the mess in the first place. Changing how you approach credit can repair your credit score and establish positive financial habits that create lasting change in your ability to manage your money responsibly. Moreover, it would make it easier for you to keep up with your bills during unexpected life events.

In *Credit Repair Tactical Guide,* you will learn how to bring a subprime credit score up to a good, great, or even excellent one. You'll determine the best action plan for your unique situation and how to implement this action plan to achieve actual results. You'll also learn valuable tips for avoiding future credit disasters so you can maximize your borrowing power without getting yourself into heaps of debt.

I know what struggling with credit means, which has given me a unique insight into the best methods of improving a subpar credit score. Growing up, my mother worked three minimum wage jobs to put food on the table for her children, and she was frequently worried about debt. I wanted to learn from my mother's struggles and figure out how to prevent this precise situation from happening to myself and my family when I grew up. Because of this, I pursued a mathematics degree and a career in finance, which has helped me recover from my own debt mistakes I made as a young adult. With every debt challenge that I'd overcame and every position I held during my many years of experience in the financial industry, I learned more about the best credit practices. I also understood how people learned and changed their spending habits in order to better equip myself to share this knowledge. I don't want to just teach you how to get out of debt; I want to help you discover the right path for you that will bring you towards financial freedom.

Suppose you're struggling to make your minimum payments. In that case, if you're not currently eligible for solutions like debt consolidation or if you're feeling lost on improving your credit, this is the right book for you. Your credit score is like a report card that reflects your ability to manage debt.

With the *Credit Repair Tactical Guide,* you'll be able to ace your classes and quickly rise to the ranks of a straight-A borrower. Following this tactical guide will help you towards achieving an outstanding credit score and financial peace of mind, which is truly invaluable.

1

# WHAT THE FICO!?!

*"Take good care of your credit, and your credit will take good care of you."*

— ANONYMOUS

To conquer your credit score, you must first know the ins and outs of what your score means and how it is calculated. This means getting familiar with the most common method for calculating a credit score, known as the Fair Isaac Corporation (FICO) score.

Think of your FICO score as a three-digit number representing how good of a borrower you are in the eyes of a credit company. When creditors lend you money, they want to know you'll pay them back, so they don't have to waste time and resources trying to collect on your debts. Therefore, they are most likely to prioritize people who have a history of repaying the money they borrow. If you fail to repay your money, or if you don't have an adequate history for these companies to make an informed judgment of your borrowing habits, there's a good chance they may refuse to work with you. Of course, the situations that lead to a poor credit score are often complicated and can frequently reflect periods of hardship in your life. You may be a model borrower under ordinary circumstances, but an unexpected event like losing your job might have led you to falling behind on your payments.

The unfortunate truth is that credit bureaus and loan companies aren't always privy to this information. Even if they knew about it, they may not be especially sympathetic, particularly if they don't believe they'll make their money back after lending to you. Because of this, your credit score serves as a quick and easy way for lenders to judge your credit history and make a decision about working with you, so it's critical to keep your score as high as possible.

To maximize your credit score, you must first know what goes into calculating these scores and how they are judged. Understanding the FICO score calculation method will give you invaluable insight into your credit score so you can start making decisions that benefit your score and, ultimately, your financial security.

## UNDERSTANDING YOUR CREDIT SCORE

The first step in fixing your credit score is to get an accurate estimate of how much work you'll need to do to bring your score up to an acceptable number. FICO credit scores can range from a low end of 300 to a high end of 850. In general, scores above 670 are considered relatively good scores, which show lenders that you are a trustworthy borrower. Ideally, you want to bring your score above this level so you can qualify for the best deals and loan interest rates. Lower scores, specifically those below 600, may prohibit you from getting these ideal rates. Scores in the poor range, generally considered to be lower than 500, reflect a rocky borrowing history. These scores tell lenders you may not be able to repay them, so these companies are less likely to let you take out a line of credit.

One matter that complicates credit scores somewhat is that they aren't calculated by a single company but rather by three different companies: the credit bureaus Experian, Transunion, and Equifax. Some lenders may not check your credit with all of these bureaus, and while your score shouldn't be too different from one company to another, there are still variations in how each of the three major credit bureaus calculates your score that can affect the end result.

### *How Credit Bureaus Work*

A credit bureau is, in essence, a company that collects and stores credit history information on millions of people. This information is compiled into reports, calculated to yield a credit score, and then sold to lenders who inquire about the credit history of potential borrowers. Whenever you apply for a loan or a new line of credit, your lender requests your information from one or more credit bureaus. They then decide to approve or deny your application based on the information they receive.

Most of the data provided by bureaus come from reports by other lenders. When you pay or fail to pay your credit card bill, this gets reported to credit bureaus and thus added to your credit report, which positively or negatively affects your score. These records are known as tradelines, including loan type, creditor name, open date, the date of last activity, outstanding balance, maximum balance, account status, amount past due (if any), minimum payment, previous payment amount, and any comments. All of these helps paint a complete picture of your track record as a borrower and your current financial situation. In addition to tradelines, some basic identifying information like your name and social security number are also present. To avoid discrimination by lenders, bureaus do not report information about your race or ethnicity, gender, or political leanings. Contrary to popular belief, financial data unrelated to loan payments like bounced checks and income are also not reported, and these factors don't affect your credit score.

***Understanding Your Report***

The rules you must follow to achieve good credit are reasonably consistent across the three bureaus. In particular, the most important factor regardless of the company calculating your score is that you pay off your debts on time while not missing payments. Every time you are late on a payment, your credit score takes a hit. What starts as a minor penalty can quickly become a huge problem, as one missed payment balloons into a series of late fees and overdrawn accounts, which can leave you feeling backed into a corner. The result is strenuous on your mental health and an equally severe toll on your credit score to match.

Other aspects of your credit score can vary in importance and the calculation method depending on the credit bureau. Factors like your total amount owed or credit usage, the length of your credit history, your credit mix, and the number of recent hard inquiries or new lines of credit all affect your credit score. Still, each bureau turns this complex data into a score with a slightly different calculation method. These companies also create their own reports of your credit history when a lender wants to verify your creditworthiness, which can differ in presentation. Therefore, while the things you need to do to get or maintain a good credit score are generally the same across all three bureaus, your score can still vary a little. Having a varying score amongst these is normal and not something to be concerned about. Unless the differences are significant, in which case there may be incorrect or missing records at one of the bureaus, you will need to address them as you work to repair your score.

The best way to keep a lookout on your credit usage track record and watch out for potential errors that could harm your score is to periodically check your credit report. Most people have a decent idea of their credit score since it is easier to check this number, and many websites and apps will let you do it for free without harming your score. However, a credit score doesn't give you nearly as much information as a report. Your score is a decent way to get a surface-level idea of how healthy your credit is, but your credit report provides you with more specific details that can give you greater insight into what is affecting your score.

You can obtain a free copy of your credit report from each of the three bureaus once per year. The simplest way to get these reports is to use freecreditreport.com, but you can also request them directly from each bureau. Your credit report allows you to keep track of the different lines of credit you have open, and it shows you relevant information like your payment history. The more information you can get about the factors that contribute to your credit score, precisely where you might be going wrong, the easier it will be for you to repair your credit, as you'll know where to focus your efforts and how to play to your strengths.

## WHICH BUREAU MATTERS MOST?

Since credit scores can differ between bureaus, it's only natural to wonder which score you should prioritize. The answer isn't as simple as just picking Experian, TransUnion, or Equifax. That's because different lenders don't always use all three bureaus. A given loan company might check your credit history through just one of the three bureaus, or they might consider multiple credit reports. Therefore, it's necessary to ensure your credit history is accurately reported across each of the three bureaus by requesting a free copy of your information every year and checking your credit score from each bureau semi-regularly.

Additionally, some bureaus calculate scores using the FICO model, while others use alternate methods, such as the VantageScore model. VantageScore was initially developed jointly by the three bureaus, so specific lenders use it, but FICO remains the most popular scoring method by far. If you're looking to improve your credit, focus on improving your FICO score first and foremost. You can get a free FICO score directly from the Experian website. Though TransUnion and Equifax do not offer this same service for free, many third-party companies allow you to check your credit score with each bureau without fees and without harming your score.

Most companies' prioritization of the FICO model is convenient because you only have to focus your efforts on improving one number. However, there are certain limitations to this strategy. The most significant is that lenders in the mortgage industry have specific cut-offs for FICO score minimums to pass approval. Having a score below their threshold, by even one point, will result in rejection regardless of your personal situation. Some companies tend only to check the number and not the actual history behind it. Because of this, two people with very different credit histories could have the same score and be treated the same way by a lender. Suppose you have an overall good record, but your score suffered when you had a financial emergency. In that case, lenders might assume you're unlikely to pay them back - resulting in denying your applications, even once you're able to get the rest of your financial situation back on track.

While FICO scores tend to paint an incomplete picture, the good news is that this tendency to only look at your credit score when evaluating your creditworthiness can also be advantageous to you. If you can improve your score, most lenders won't care that you struggled to pay your bills in the past, as long as they believe you can pay off your debts now. Credit repair can be your pathway to a life free of financial worries and stress. The sooner you start revamping your borrowing habits, the sooner you will qualify for better loan rates, and the easier it will be for you to remain in good financial standing.

## OPTIONS FOR DEALING WITH POOR CREDIT

A low credit score doesn't need to hold you back forever. You have many options available that can help you experience a debt-free and stress-free life. The best choice for you will depend on multiple factors, including your current income, the extent of your debts, your credit score, your life situation, and your personal preference. The four best routes available to you moving forward are credit counseling, debt settlement, credit repair, and bankruptcy.

***Credit Counseling***

Credit counseling is often the first step people take when they get in over their heads with debt or don't know where to begin when they have a poor credit score. It is the least drastic of all the possible options, as it primarily involves education about sound financial practices and available resources. However, it is still very effective for many people experiencing mild to moderate challenges regarding their credit scores.

A common reason people find themselves in debt is that they were never taught to handle credit properly, such as overspending on credit cards, taking out too many loans at a time, or being unaware of how quickly interest can build up. Maybe they have all of their debts carefully balanced without any sort of safety net, and one minor emergency like an auto repair or a health scare depletes their available income. Then they are blindsided by bills they can't afford, which only worsen over time, digging them deeper and deeper into a debt hole. If this sounds familiar, you're certainly not alone, as very few people have access to adequate credit education before they get credit cards of their own.

Credit counseling fills in any gaps in knowledge you may have about proper credit usage and money management, helping you develop healthier and more fiscally responsible habits. These habits assist in repairing your score and make it less likely you will have similar issues with your credit usage in the future.

Proper credit counseling can be invaluable, so I find it deeply important that everyone is able to access the understanding to manage their money better. I offer free financial education services; you can opt into my mailing list on my website https://allenanything.com and send me an email asking to schedule a one-on-one call with me or someone on my team. We focus on developing clients' knowledge of money matters by analyzing their current personal financial situation. It's also why I write books for anyone looking to improve their financial literacy across many areas. Through education about important topics like budgeting, debt management, and debt consolidation, you *can* turn your life around and ease any money troubles.

Budgeting seems like a simple tool, but it is more effective than you may think at first. Learning to budget is about much more than simply making a few spreadsheets. It is about developing a better understanding of where your money goes and identifying areas where you are spending excessively and should cut back.

Creating a budget and sticking to it can make it easier to pay your bills each month and stay on top of any outstanding debts until they are completely paid off. It can also improve your saving habits, as you have more money left over each month to tuck away for a rainy day, which prevents future emergencies from breaking the bank.

Once you understand how to budget, you can begin to work toward debt management. Paying off your debts may feel impossible sometimes, but it isn't nearly as hard as it seems with the proper resources and knowledge. Debt management strategies can make a huge difference in your ability to repair your credit even if you don't have the highest income. Developing a new repayment plan is a great way to compound the positive change you're already making by budgeting, ensuring you can pay off your debts faster without overwhelming yourself financially or mentally.

One closing topic touched on in credit counseling is debt consolidation, which takes out a single loan to pay for many different debts. Consolidation allows you to focus on repaying just one loan at a time, often with a lower interest rate and monthly minimum payments. Many people find consolidated debts far easier to pay, mainly when applying budgeting and debt management methods. If you're interested in learning more about debt consolidation and whether it might be the right move for you, check out my book *Make a Payment* for more information and a more detailed consolidation guide.

***Debt Settlement***

If you have a good deal of outstanding debt and you don't think you'll be able to pay it off, even with a payment plan, then debt settlement may be the right path for you. Debt settlement refers to a process where you and your lender agree on a repayment amount less than what you currently owe them. Your lender wants to get at least some portion of their money back, and many creditors are willing to accept less than what they are owed now rather than waiting for a future payout that may or may not happen.

While debt settlements sound like a dream come true, they too come with their issues. For one, debt settlements can still be costly, and they require that you have some money upfront to pay off at least a portion of your current debt. If you don't have enough money in your savings to put a dent in what you owe, it's unlikely a creditor will accept your settlement proposal. Another issue is that agreeing on settlement terms can take quite a long time, and it can be challenging to navigate if you don't know what you're doing. Luckily, this book is here to help. In Chapter 3, we'll go over debt settlement in more detail, including the steps you need to take if you want to work with lenders to settle your debts.

While significant barriers like time and your savings can prevent debt settlement from being the perfect path for everyone, it's still a handy tool for digging yourself out of debt that is harming your credit. Getting rid of your debts is the first step to getting back on track with on-time payments, which is the most effective way to improve your credit score. Debt settlement serves as a partial reset without the rippling repercussions of declaring bankruptcy, as long as you have the money and patience necessary for it.

### *Credit Repair*

Debt settlement and credit counseling are only half the battle on the path to financial freedom. Ultimately, there is no fast and easy way to fix bad credit. You can only accomplish real positive change by examining your spending and saving habits, identifying your weak points, and working to replace bad habits with better ones that allow you to pay off your debts on time in the future. The credit repair pathway isn't especially novel, but it is a fairly straightforward method for improving your credit score regardless of your income level and debt situation.

There are many methods available to you to start improving your credit score, especially if inaccuracies are harming your score in your credit reports. You can learn to use the free resources at your disposal, like annual credit reports from the major bureaus, to identify mistakes and revamp your borrowing habits. You can use third-party software to help you better understand your credit report and get inaccurate information removed from these reports. You can even pay for the services of a credit repair company, which will act on your behalf to dispute negative information on your credit report. In any case, credit repair must be followed by a fundamental change in your financial habits; otherwise, the benefits will not last for long. Once your credit reports are cleared of any incorrect items, prevent any future issues by routinely making on-time payments and ensuring you are contributing to your savings. You can find more information about credit repair in Chapter 4 that will help guide you through the process.

***Bankruptcy***

Bankruptcy is generally considered a last-resort move because it can have serious consequences that aren't worth it if you can repair your credit another way. It's often painted as the easy way out of debt in theory, but in practice, it is riskier. Depending on the type of bankruptcy you declare, you may still be responsible for paying some of your debts, and your credit score could be negatively impacted for years to come. Still, despite its drawbacks, bankruptcy is sometimes the best option available to you. Whether you think you may need to declare bankruptcy or not, it is worth learning more about what the process entails and its risks and benefits, which will be explained toward the end of the book.

Credit counseling, debt settlement, credit repair, and bankruptcy will all be covered in future chapters. Read about each one in more detail and decide which plan best suits your situation as you work toward achieving relief from debt. Credit counseling is a phenomenal starting place if you just need to put yourself on the right path and adjust your spending and saving habits. If you have more outstanding debts than you can reasonably pay off, learning more about debt settlement can help you navigate these uncertain waters. If your credit score is deficient and you aren't sure what to do to fix it, focus on credit repair. If you find you're really in a bind, and you have exhausted all other options, then you may need to read up on how to declare bankruptcy so you can navigate these uncertain waters without making your situation any worse. Keep in mind that you may be able to use more than one of these options, so it's worth taking the time to learn about each of them before you make your next move.

Once you've chosen a pathway, the only thing left is to follow through on the advice and execute it. The work will be well worth it, as repairing your credit will finally help you achieve financial peace of mind. You may need a simple solution like forming and following good money habits or a more in-depth one like declaring bankruptcy. Nothing will get better if you don't take action. Start improving your credit today so you can enjoy a better future.

# 2

# CREDIT COUNSELING

*"No one can make you feel inferior without your consent."*

— ELEANOR ROOSEVELT

The reality of excessive debt and a poor credit score can be difficult pills to swallow. Getting into debt is all too easy, but getting out of it can mean a tough upward climb. It can take anywhere from months to years to fully repair your credit. Though the effort you expend is worth the final result, this process can take even longer if you don't have a good idea of the kinds of bad practices and harmful habits that got you into trouble with your credit in the first place.

Credit counseling is an integral part of credit repair because it teaches you how to bring your score up and keep it high for the foreseeable future. A little advice goes a long way if you're willing to take a critical eye to your spending habits and revise how you use credit so you can avoid racking up debt in the future. However, despite its usefulness, many people have reservations about talking to a credit counselor that prevents them from getting the help they need to fix their credit.

Even though just about everyone will need to learn how to manage money in their lifetime, financial education is consistently lacking in schools across the nation. It's common to graduate high school with little to no idea on how to prepare your taxes, create a budget, or use credit responsibly. This financial education gap may seem trivial, but it has real consequences on how much debt Americans get into every year. According to a study conducted by the U. S. Federal Reserve, nearly 40% of adults would not be able to cover the bill if presented with an unexpected expense of merely $400. The need to sell something or borrow money would be their only option. This statistic points to a startling lack of financial literacy among Americans, preventing people from developing good habits with their money.

Few people can contribute enough money to their savings to cover even moderate financial emergencies, which means the average American is reliant on credit for unexpected expenses, contributing to worsening debt.

The most effective long-term strategy for reducing debt and improving your credit score is financial education, specifically through credit counseling. While being born into money or securing a high-paying job can help you keep expenses down, having a surplus of cash prevents you from burning through it on unnecessary costs and lousy borrowing habits. Even if you win the lottery, you can just as quickly spend all that money and end up in debt once again. So, it doesn't matter how much money you earn. You can still have money troubles if you don't develop good financial habits. Credit counseling provides you with the knowledge you need to equip yourself to dig yourself out of credit troubles and prevent yourself from falling into the same pitfalls in the future. Education forms the basis of good habits, which will keep you out of trouble and help you navigate future unexpected emergencies without racking up a credit card bill. If you didn't have the opportunity to learn good spending habits and feel like you're paying for this gap in your knowledge now, or if you need a personalized refresher course, then credit counseling may be what you need.

## WHAT IS CREDIT COUNSELING?

Credit counseling is a service typically provided by non-profit organizations and individuals who are well-versed in financial coaching practices. Most counselors are trained and certified in the realm of budgeting, consumer credit, and debt management, so they can best help identify the areas you need support with and guide you toward finding the best solution for your current situation. The purpose of a credit counselor is not to lecture you on why you're handling your money wrong or to shame you for mistakes and events that were out of your control. Instead, the primary purpose of attending credit counseling is to find a solution to the current problem. Credit counselors provide long-term advice you can use when making decisions about your money for years to come, so even if you're not in immediate trouble with your credit or savings, it may still be worth seeking out their services.

Credit counselors will sit down with you in a one-on-one personalized setting. They will review your financial situation to help you better understand where you are right now and what factors contributed to your current situation. This meeting allows them to provide more practical advice. For example, someone who gets into debt due to out-of-control spending habits will benefit from a different direction than someone who missed some credit card payments because they had a medical emergency that drained their bank account. Therefore, the first step in any credit counseling program is for the counselor to learn about your credit history and decide what services would benefit you the most.

Most credit counselors provide a wide range of services to help you get back on track with your finances. These services typically begin with advice on how you can develop better habits with your money, turning incremental changes that are easy to implement into a long-lasting positive impact on your bank account and your credit score. Credit counselors can guide you through reviewing your credit score and credit report to identify potential problems and weaknesses. They can assist you in learning how to better manage your money, typically through the use of a budget and a dedicated saving strategy. In some cases, they may provide you with free or low-cost educational resources, such as pamphlets and workshops, with additional credit advice. Generally, most counselors will also assist you in creating a plan for paying down your debts and working toward improving your credit score. They can create a personalized strategy that is well-suited to your individual needs, which makes credit counseling a potent tool when you're looking for the best way to repair your credit.

Note that most of the benefits of credit counseling are long-term ones, with minimal short-term impact. Your debts aren't going to disappear after one or two meetings instantly. Credit counselors usually can't do much to raise your credit score immediately unless there are significant errors on your credit report. However, just because you might not get instant relief, this doesn't mean you should throw out the idea of meeting with a credit counselor entirely. On the contrary, as long as you properly manage your expectations and approach your meeting with a counselor with an open mind, you'll find that this long-term approach is much more effective in preventing future problems with credit.

### *Finding a Reputable Credit Counselor*

Not all credit counseling services are created equal. While the vast majority of credit counselors operate as a non-profit business, this doesn't necessarily mean their services are free, nor does it mean that every credit counselor offers the same quality of advice. When selecting the credit counselor you want to work with, you'll undoubtedly want to see if they are adequately trained and certified. You wouldn't take financial advice from just anybody, and you want to make sure you're not paying for faulty suggestions from someone who doesn't really know what they're talking about. Certification is the bare minimum requirement you should look for when judging a given counselor's reputability.

Keep a wary eye out for red flags, such as counseling agencies that offer little to no information about the kind and extent of the services they provide. You shouldn't need to provide your personal information to learn about their services either. While you will need to discuss your financial history when you start working with a credit counselor, basic information about the counselor's services should be publicly available.

The final area of concern comes in the form of hidden fees. The last thing you want to do right now is to get into any more debt. Many reputable credit counselors charge for their services, but these costs should be reasonable, and the counselor should be upfront about them. Disreputable businesses may attempt to hide their high fees, which is a red flag in just about every industry. Before you settle on a credit counselor, do some research into the company or individual providing the services, and see what other people who previously worked with them have to say. Once you've completed the vetting process and found a counselor you can trust, you'll find it much easier to take their advice, which can help you avoid having to resort to drastic measures like declaring bankruptcy.

***Avoiding Bankruptcy***

One of the primary goals of attending credit counseling is to avoid being forced to declare bankruptcy. Many people view bankruptcy as a quick and easy way to get out of debt, eliminating their responsibility to pay back what they owe and giving them a fresh start. While this is a widespread perception, especially among people who have been struggling with debt for a long time, unfortunately, it only comes from looking at bankruptcy through rose-colored lenses. The reality of declaring bankruptcy is that it is a complicated and often messy process that may or may not remove all of your debts. Even if your debts are entirely cleared, going bankrupt can still have a long-lasting negative impact on your credit. Hence, most credit counselors advise pursuing it only as a last resort when all of your other options have been exhausted. When you work with a credit counselor, they will help you find solutions for dealing with debt and a low credit score that doesn't involve bankruptcy. While avoiding bankruptcy may not always be possible, depending on your situation, but meeting with a credit counselor should be your first step before you consider more drastic measures for repairing your credit.

To better understand credit counseling, it helps to understand what differentiates it from bankruptcy and how it differs from other options for improving your credit, such as debt settlement and credit repair. By breaking down each method and comparing them to credit counseling, you can make a more informed decision about which pathway is best suited for you.

## CREDIT COUNSELING VERSUS DEBT SETTLEMENT

When you want to improve your credit, debt settlement and credit counseling are both valuable options available to you. However, they each have their own strengths and weaknesses that make them better suited to different situations. Generally speaking, credit counseling is a less extreme option that's best suited to people with moderate amounts of debt. It is ideal as a preventative solution or as a way to course-correct before you end up with mountains of debt you can't afford to pay off. Alternatively, debt settlement is best suited to situations where your debt has grown so out of hand that you cannot keep up with regular payments. The longer a debt goes unpaid, the less effective credit counseling will be on its own, though it can still be combined with other forms of debt management in a comprehensive credit repair strategy.

Everyone's debt situation is different, so it's essential to understand the differences between these two methods so you can decide on the best plan of attack for you. Three key areas to keep in mind when choosing between credit counseling and debt settlement are the effects each method has on your credit score, how they help you resolve debts, and their long-term gains and drawbacks.

***Changes to Your Credit Score***

Both credit counseling and debt settlements are meant to improve your credit in the long run, but it is still possible to harm your credit in some cases, even if the setback is only temporary. For credit counseling, this risk comes into play because debt relief is not immediate. If you decide to pursue credit counseling when you have a lot of outstanding debt, you will still have to pay that debt off. You will likely shorten your repayment period if you follow the advice you receive, but this advice isn't a cure-all for your debt problems. Still, working with a credit counselor will eventually allow you to reach the end of the debt tunnel. Gradually bringing up your credit score with each on-time payment makes credit counseling a safe bet if you're looking to raise or maintain your score.

Debt settlement, on the other hand, can create unavoidable penalties that lower your score. When you settle a debt, this is marked down on your credit score. You won't have to pay as much money, but lenders don't like to see that you have too many settled debts, as this implies they may not get all of their money back if they let you take out a new loan or line of credit. Settled debts are negatively scored by all the models that determine your credit score, and this negative impact will persist on your report for seven years from the settlement date, making it a harsh penalty to shake. Even if you can get your finances in order and avoid going into debt again, you still might not qualify for the best loan and credit rates until this charge falls off your report.

Additionally, debt settlement companies cannot help until a debt becomes delinquent. Because of this, they may advise you to purposefully stop paying a loan so they can negotiate a cheaper settlement for you. Any late or missed payments can harm your credit score, so your number may drop even lower during the process of debt settlement and for quite a while after. Therefore, while debt settlements provide more rapid debt relief, you should seriously consider their potential long-term drawbacks before deciding if it's the right path for you.

***Debt Management and Settlement***

While debt management and debt settlement may sound the same, and they share a similar goal of helping you eliminate outstanding debts, the two processes are very different, and they can have vastly different effects. When you pursue a debt settlement, you're typically looking for a way to resolve an outstanding delinquent debt that you are unlikely to be able to pay off in full. Most companies will not consider settling a debt until it has been marked as delinquent for a period, which can range from a few months to a few years. Additionally, as mentioned above, settlements can harm your credit score temporarily. Even though these penalties eventually fall off your credit report, they can still cause problems for you for a few years if you apply for a loan or a new line of credit.

Credit counselors pursue a different kind of debt reduction plan known as debt management. Your credit counselor will work with your lender to renegotiate the terms of your loan. You will typically still have to pay the entire balance plus any additional interest that accrues in the meantime, so if you are no longer in a position where that's financially viable, this method may not be for you. However, credit counselors may be able to secure you lower monthly payments in exchange for a more extended repayment period, which many people find to be far more feasible even at lower income levels. You may not be able to afford to pay $400 a month for two years, but paying the same amount in $200 a month increments for eight years could be much easier to keep up with. In other cases, your credit counselor may be able to secure a lower interest rate, so you end up paying less in the long run.

In some cases, you may even be eligible for a temporary grace period based on your income, depending on the type of loan in question. This option is usually only available for government loans such as federal student loans. Still, if you qualify, this grace period can be integral to helping you get back on your feet so you can adequately pay down your debts at a later date.

Both debt management and debt settlement can be helpful in different situations. Still, debt management gives you more control over your repayment plan and helps you avoid some of the pitfalls of the settlement method. Since loans aren't marked as settled on your credit report and instead get repaid in full, the penalties to your credit score are lower as long as you can keep up with the payments. You can renegotiate the terms of significant debts before they become overwhelming, which means you're able to proactively handle potential problems before they can harm your credit score. Perhaps most importantly, you also receive invaluable insight into better methods for loan repayment, which can make a world of difference for how you choose to approach the use of credit in the future.

### *Long-Term Benefits*

The final reason you might be more inclined to choose credit counseling over debt settlement is that credit counseling provides a pathway for tremendous long-term success in using credit responsibly. Let's say you settle all of your debts and you don't owe anything anymore. This is an opportunity for a fresh start, but it's effortless to make the same mistakes that got you into a mess with debt in the first place. In a few years, you could find yourself stuck in the same situation, once again having to resort to debt settlement to dig yourself out of the hole. You may have been free from your struggles with debt, but you didn't learn how to manage your money better, so there's a good chance you'll end up right back where you started.

Better financial education in the form of credit counseling can help resolve this issue. Working with a counselor teaches you where you went wrong and what you need to do to get yourself back on the right track. You learn how to take greater responsibility in managing your money. Better yet, if you ever do get yourself into debt again after paying it all off, you know how to get yourself out of it rather than having to rely on a debt settler. Not to say that debt settling is inherently wrong, of course. When used correctly and responsibly, debt settlements can be precisely what you need to take back control of your credit. But to make long-lasting changes in the way you handle money, consider also setting up a credit counseling appointment, which lowers the risk of ending up with piles of debt once again. Combining debt settlement and credit counseling can be an especially powerful tool that will help you get out of debt in the present, as well as avoid debt in the future.

## CREDIT COUNSELING VERSUS CREDIT REPAIR

While credit counseling focuses primarily on changing bad habits into good ones to gradually improve your credit score, credit repair takes a more direct approach. Credit repair services help to identify and scrub clean any incorrectly reported items on your credit report that could be holding your score back. These include mistakenly labeled missed payments, incorrect dates, inaccurate loan balances, and any other penalty to your credit that shouldn't be on your report. According to the Consumer Financial Protection Bureau, credit repair cannot wipe away genuinely missed payments, but it can help fix mistakes that affect around 20% of all credit reports. A credit repair company can also correct information that is the product of identity fraud or items from someone else's information filed under your name unintentionally.

While it is vital to review your credit report for errors, as discussed in the previous chapter, credit repair services have pros and cons that help to differentiate them from the benefits and limitations of standard credit counseling. Familiarize yourself with the differences between these approaches to decide the best choice for your situation.

### *Convenience of Service*

Credit repair services are very convenient because you, the borrower, don't have to do much to see your credit score improve. You can pay a company to do all the hard work of reviewing your credit reports, locating potential errors, and filing the necessary paperwork to get these errors verified and removed from your reports. Once you pay a company to review your credit, the task is out of your hands, which makes this a very appealing option for people who don't have the time to sit down and read through each item in their credit reports themselves. This differs from credit counseling, which usually involves multiple meetings with a counselor to create and enact a plan to improve your credit. Credit counseling is a more involved process; you can't pay someone else to fix your bad habits for you, so you must have the time necessary to put in the work if you want to see results.

At the same time, it's important to note that credit repair companies aren't doing anything you couldn't do yourself. They are simply reviewing your reports and notifying credit bureaus of any issues, filing all the same paperwork you would need to do if you decided to take matters into your own hands. Not everyone has the time or willingness to sit down and double-check every negative line on their credit reports, which makes credit repair an attractive option. But for those who value their money more, it is entirely possible for you to perform the same tasks that a credit repair company would have completed in your stead. You only need to decide whether the price is worth saving the energy and time involved.

***Cost Considerations***

Most credit counselors operate on a non-profit basis, which makes credit counseling a very affordable option. The last thing you want to do is get yourself into more unnecessary debt when you're already trying to pay off what you owe. Rudimentary credit counseling services are often cheap or free, while more advanced services like creating a debt management payment plan can come with nominal fees. In general, though, credit counseling is affordable and effective, even if there's little chance you will see any instant results.

While credit repair is more likely to provide the instant results you might be looking for, the companies that offer these services are typically for-profit. Some may charge a flat fee or only charge you once a negative item has been successfully disputed and removed from your credit report. However, it's more common for companies to charge a monthly fee similar to a subscription service, which lasts until the company has reviewed your entire credit report. The costs and lengths of time most people pay for credit repair services vary depending on service type. Still, according to a survey conducted by Intuit, customers pay an average of $64 per month for approximately 13 months, totaling $832 for a credit repair service. Keep in mind this is an average, and the saying goes, "you get what you pay for," so don't dismiss a service if they charge more than the average. That being said, a credit repair service can be a hefty bill if you haven't saved up enough for it, and you don't want to get yourself into further debt. If you don't have much money in your savings, it may be more cost-effective to stick to less expensive services like credit counseling and to perform a credit report check on your own.

On the other hand, credit repair companies often have access to more time, money, experience, and resources, so they may catch errors you might miss. You might decide the price tag is worth the added certainty that professional companies, like The Financial ER (https://thefinancialer.com), will readily recognize mistakes on your report due to their level of experience. Choosing to go with a credit repair company will ultimately depend on your financial situation.

***Potential for No Change***

The final thing to remember about credit repair services is that no guarantee paying for them will bring up your credit score. While millions of people have errors on their credit reports that could be harming their FICO scores, millions more have low scores caused by regular late payments and other complications that may not be removed. Credit repair services can only do something about incorrect items on your credit report, and they cannot erase previous mistakes. The result is that you pay for assistance with a chance they may not help you outside of just credit counseling.

With solely a credit counseling service, everyone can benefit from learning more about managing their money and handling debt responsibly, no matter their current financial situation and credit score. When you sign up for credit counseling, you're sure to learn something new that could make a big difference in how you approach credit in the future. With credit repair, there are no guarantees, which could be a relatively useless service for you depending on whether or not there are any errors to correct or if the company also provides additional services.

Like with debt settlement, if you are interested in utilizing credit repair services and think they can help, it is a good idea to brush up on your knowledge with some credit counseling. Once you know your credit report has a clean bill of health, you can hone in on any problem areas in your spending and saving habits. The only organic method to remove the effect of negative items on your report is to outweigh them with positive ones. Outside of making payments on time, the best way to achieve this is through credit counseling. If you cannot learn to manage credit responsibly, or if your debts get too severe due to a financial emergency, you may have to resort to declaring bankruptcy instead.

## CREDIT COUNSELING VERSUS BANKRUPTCY

Bankruptcy is one of the most misunderstood methods of credit restoration. It is often misrepresented as a magical process that will wash away your debt and wipe your slate clean so that you can have a perfect credit score. In reality, many of these beliefs about bankruptcy are simply myths painting a picture that is too good to be true. Bankruptcy can do a great deal of harm to your credit score before it recovers, and many lenders won't approve applications from anyone who has recently declared bankruptcy. When used responsibly, bankruptcy can serve as a last-resort measure, so it's important to consider other options like credit counseling first.

Many people forego credit counseling in favor of pursuing bankruptcy. Still, since bankruptcy is such an extreme measure, it should only be on the table when you have exhausted all other methods of fixing your credit. There is no easy way to undo filing for bankruptcy, and unlike credit counseling, it doesn't always help you avoid racking up new debts in the future. This isn't to say that you should never explore bankruptcy, but only that it is more of a last resort than traditional counseling. Carefully consider the short-term and long-term effects of both of these options for credit repair before you rush to declare bankruptcy, or you could end up worse off than where you began.

***Mandatory Credit Counseling***

According to federal law, anyone who files for bankruptcy must also complete a credit counseling course. The goal is to prevent you from falling into the same pitfalls and having to declare bankruptcy for a second time. Because of this, bankruptcy has a leg up over credit repair and debt settlement services because you still have the opportunity to learn key skills that will lower the likelihood of having credit issues in the future. At the same time, if you want the benefits of credit counseling, you don't have to go through bankruptcy to get them. Credit counseling services are available to any and everyone. If you aren't in too much debt, you may be able to forego bankruptcy entirely and improve your debt situation on your own, using what you've learned from counseling.

Note that you are still responsible for paying your debts off yourself under normal circumstances while working with a credit counselor. If you choose to pursue bankruptcy alongside credit counseling, you won't have to pay off some or all of these debts. You can start saving up and applying for new lines of credit, though keep in mind that lenders may not be rushing to approve your applications. Nevertheless, if your debts are too much to manage on your own, bankruptcy may be the only way for you to get back on your feet.

***Benefits and Drawbacks of Bankruptcy***

It can be a good idea to declare bankruptcy in certain circumstances, even if you plan to utilize credit counseling anyway. While bankruptcy is a more extreme solution than other options like debt settlement, it does come with the benefit that you don't have to seek creditors' approval. Instead, a judge decides what portion of your assets are divided among each creditor based on what you owe. While this does mean it's more difficult to negotiate how much you'll pay to settle the debts, it also means you won't get stuck in a back-and-forth situation with lenders and your debt settlement company. These negotiations could last for multiple months, draining your wallet in the process.

The most significant benefit of bankruptcy is that it is one of the few options that can truly free you from the stresses of keeping up with your debts all at once. Bankruptcy settles any and all unsecured debts you have. Secured debts are backed by collateral should you fail to pay them back. These include home and auto loans, where lenders can repossess your house or car if you miss too many payments. In most cases, secured debts are not removed just because you declare bankruptcy. However, all unsecured debts are erased, and these include personal loans, credit card balances, and medical bills. Unsecured debts tend to have higher interest rates and are therefore more devastating when you miss payments, which means that even clearing up these debts can put you in a much better position to handle your secured loans. When you are no longer being hounded by endless calls from collections agencies and increasingly insistent creditors, you can take full advantage of the opportunity that bankruptcy provides to restore your credit.

Unfortunately, bankruptcy also has many drawbacks that may make it a less than ideal solution for your situation. Once you file bankruptcy, it can last for a decade on your credit report. During this time, you will have more trouble qualifying for loans and lines of credit, which could make it tough to start rebuilding your credit. While bankruptcy's negative impact on your score does decrease over time, you aren't going to qualify for the best loan rates for quite a few years. You may also be unable to move for a while, as your credit score could drop low enough that you're unable to get a mortgage or even approval for renting an apartment. You should carefully consider how filing for bankruptcy might interfere with your future plans before you make a decade-long commitment that could have dire consequences.

Another potential issue comes in the form of employment. Bankruptcy records are public, which means they come up when a company runs a background check prior to offering you a job. Some employers may be less likely to hire you if they believe you have financial problems, in part due to the negative stigma surrounding bankruptcy. Even though the grievous debt is most often the result of an unforeseen expense rather than any moral failing, many people don't see it this way. Learning you had to file for bankruptcy could cause them to view you as being irresponsible. If you're worried about your job prospects, you may want to see if you can resolve your problems with other forms of debt management to avoid this negative stigma.

Bankruptcy may not wipe away all of your debts and it may also leave a lasting mark on your credit, but it doesn't doom you to a life of poor credit forever. On the contrary, when used responsibly and with full knowledge of what bankruptcy does and doesn't do, it provides you with a chance to start rebuilding your credit from the ground up. Once the debt burden is lifted off your back, you can put the lessons you have learned in credit counseling to good use and steadily increase your credit score with repeated on-time payments. Some people can qualify for large loans like mortgages again in just a few years. Still, you'll want to be extra confident that bankruptcy is the right move for you before you proceed so you can avoid any unnecessary drawbacks.

### *How to Choose Between Your Options*

Now that you have a good idea of your options and how they differ, you can start to decide which pathway is best for you. There is no single method for getting out of debt and improving your credit score. Everyone takes a slightly different path, and what works for one person may not work for everyone else. Some people may only need to work with a credit counselor, while others require a more aggressive plan for dealing with their debt like settlement or bankruptcy. Identify the method that works for you, starting by reviewing your current debt and repayment options.

Generally, each method of debt management is best suited for a different level of debt. If you have missed a few payments, but you haven't had any serious issues with debt, and you're just looking to raise your score a few dozen points to qualify for better interest rates, then you may only need credit counseling. Even with poor credit, if you have minimal debts now and the negative items on your credit report come from past issues, more aggressive options may not benefit you. Alternatively, if you believe there may be errors in your report bringing your credit score down, then a credit repair service would be especially useful.

On the other hand, if you're struggling with a lot of debt, you will need to choose an option that helps you quickly rid yourself of that debt before it can continue to harm your credit. Debt settlement is the best choice if you don't think you can pay your debts off in full by yourself, but you have some money saved up to make partial payments. Remember that you will still need to pay at least a portion of what you owe to settle each loan, though working with a debt settlement agency can bring the costs down significantly. If you cannot afford to make settlement payments and you feel like your debt is entirely overwhelming, then bankruptcy may be the right choice for you, as long as you have carefully considered the long-term benefits and drawbacks.

The good news is that all debt management plans can benefit from credit counseling. Attending counseling is the most affordable option as well as the most reliable. Even if it doesn't solve all of your problems, you will still learn valuable information about creating a debt repayment plan, saving money in case of an emergency, and how to repair your credit over time. You can then combine these lessons with debt settlement, credit repair, filing for bankruptcy, or working to improve your credit on your own the old-fashioned way. In any case, credit counseling serves as the cornerstone of your future financial success. The more you know, the easier it will be for you to plan and prepare for emergencies, and the faster you can raise your credit score.

# 3

# DEBT SETTLEMENT

*"Instead of doing the best thing, we sometimes have to settle for the rightest thing."*

— JODI PICOULT

Under ideal circumstances, you should be able to pay off all your debts comfortably, either paying them in full or continuing to make recurring payments on time to prevent racking up excessive debt and harming your credit score. If you're falling behind on your payments, a few adjustments in your spending and saving habits should resolve the issue and allow you to bring your score back up. However, the realities of life are rarely so ideal. Whether it comes from medical expenses or out-of-control spending, significant debt can be especially devastating, even if it doesn't seem that way at first. Even smaller debts can spiral, growing more prominent over time until you're no longer able to keep up with minimum payments, let alone pay these debts off ultimately. In these circumstances, minor changes won't do the job. You'll need to take a different approach to resolve your debts while you still can, which often means settling them.

If debt settlement sounds like the right path forward for you, then you'll want to learn about the ins and outs of the process in greater detail. While settling your debts can be helpful in reducing the amount you owe and guide you towards the right track to repairing your credit, there are many ways to misuse debt settlement. For one, you may end up with the wrong settlement company that is more interested in making money than they are in actually reducing what you owe. Learn to differentiate the grifters from those genuinely interested in helping you on your financial journey, so you don't waste your time and money. It's also a good idea to avoid debt settlement without some cash in your savings or a concrete plan to save up. You'll need to be able to pay the amount of the settlement in full once an agreement is reached, and if you can't, no reputable debt settlement company is going to work with you.

Finally, have a good idea of the terms you want to negotiate based on the original loan amount and what you can afford to pay. Lenders will not accept a few hundred dollars for settlement if you owe them $20,000, but it's also a bad idea to commit to paying several thousand dollars if this would completely drain your savings and income. Negotiating for ideal terms can be difficult, which is one more reason why you need to work with the right company. In any case, the more you understand about the debt settlement process, the better off you will be as you work toward achieving financial stability.

## HOW DEBT SETTLEMENT WORKS

As mentioned in the previous chapter, debt settlement involves agreeing to pay a certain fraction of your currently existing debt in exchange for a lender forgiving the remainder of your debt. Once a debt is settled, creditors will stop contacting you about missed payments, and you won't owe any more interest on the loan or credit line. Creditors will also be unable to sue you for the remainder of the debt since the settlement is a legal agreement the company cannot violate. Because of this, settling your debts can be a huge relief that rids you of a lot of financially motivated stress. It can also put you in a better position to improve your credit. No longer having to worry about keeping up with debts that have long since become unpayable is a colossal burden to shed. After you settle, you can steadily build your credit back up over time with small, low-interest, or interest-free purchases that you pay off in full each month, providing you with a clear pathway for credit repair.

On the surface, debt settlement seems like a dream come true, but it's not always an ideal choice. It has plenty of downsides to balance out its benefits. One of the most significant is that debt settlement doesn't immediately repair your credit. In fact, it can actually make your credit much worse in the short term since debts are marked as 'settled,' which is scored negatively. It takes a lot of work to bring your credit back up once you've had to settle your debts. At the same time, settling your debts may be the only way for you to clear a pathway to better credit in the first place, so this is a downside that many people are willing to accept.

Another drawback is that debt settlement can take a long time, and you may not erase all your debts even after a few years. This can be a significant problem because these financial obligations remain delinquent during the settlement process. If it turns out that you are unable to settle them, you will be stuck paying the additional interest that has accumulated, which can sometimes make pursuing settlement risky. One study found that only 43 percent of debts are settled by the third year of the process. However, do not let this risk deter you if you are so held back by debt that you cannot see a way to pay it all off yourself.

Debt settlement can be a long and arduous process, but you can seriously cut down on what you owe if you are successful. Success is typically dependent on two factors: the quality of your negotiations, whether you contact the companies yourself or work with a debt settlement agency, and the lenders you're attempting to settle the debts with.

**Why Lenders Will Settle**

At first glance, you may be surprised to learn that lenders are willing to settle debts at all. They loaned you money believing they would make it back with interest, so why would they accept a fraction of what you owe them when they could continue to charge you interest for years? The answer becomes apparent when you consider the situation from the lender's point of view, specifically how extended periods of debt collection affect lenders financially.

First, it's important to note that not all lenders have their own in-house debt collectors. Many smaller lenders don't have the funds for this, so once a debt goes into collections, there's not much they can do about it themselves. They have to sell your debt to a dedicated debt collection agency, which is the company that then comes calling to collect these debts. The lender sells the debt to these companies at a deep discount, so any debt that enters the collections stage will already lose them some money. Also, the collections process can be draining even on larger companies that do have a collections department. They have to divert time and staffing to track you down and hound you themselves. Understandably, many companies would rather skip this hassle altogether, making them more receptive to a settlement.

Let's say you're a lender and someone owes your company $5,000. They've routinely missed payments or failed to pay enough to make any real progress on repaying the debt. This has been going on for multiple years and given what your company makes on its other customers, it hardly seems worth it to continue to pursue the debt. Then you get a letter from the debtor and they say they're willing to give you $2,000 today in exchange for forgiving the remaining $3,000 of debt. Would you take the deal? The answer is yes for many creditors since they already manage more profitable accounts and may not want to deal with your situation anymore.

As the old saying goes, a bird in the hand is worth two in the bush. If a creditor knows they're guaranteed to get $2,000 today, but there's no guarantee they'll ever get the total $5,000 back, it may be worth taking the $3,000 loss, especially if they would lose more if they sold the debt to third-party collectors. Add onto this hypothetical scenario that many lenders spend money on their efforts to get you to pay your debts. Selling your records to a debt collector typically means taking a significant loss on what they're owed, and the decision becomes effortless. Most lenders will accept getting a portion of what they're owed in exchange for no longer having to deal with attempting to collect your debt, as it isn't worth their time to continue to hold out. They're willing to accept a settlement if you can convince them they're getting a good enough deal.

Of course, this final caveat of giving the lenders a good enough deal is a sticking point in negotiations. If you can't offer enough of a lump sum to buy out your debt effectively, the lender may decide to just pass the debt along to collections instead. If you aren't able to negotiate for the most favorable settlement possible, on the other hand, you could be the one losing more money than the settlement is really worth. This is why it's so vital to choose an effective team of debt settlement experts who can get you the best possible results.

However, you should be careful to avoid spending too much on negotiations to negate the benefits of settling.

**How Cheap Is Debt Settlement?**

Debt settlement is often touted as the cheapest method of debt relief, but just how accurate is this perception? To be sure, settling a large debt for a fraction of the cost can save you a lot of money. At the same time, it's requisite to consider the other fees and payments that might raise the debt settlement cost quite a bit higher than you might assume.

The primary cause of higher-than-expected costs comes from interest and fees on the debt itself. For a debt to qualify for settlement, it must be delinquent, which means you must stop keeping up with monthly payments. If you have already stopped making payments, this won't be much of a change, but in either case, letting a debt go unpaid for an extended time isn't cheap. Fees for missed payments stack up quickly, and interest continues to compound during the debt settlement negotiations. If you aren't able to agree with the creditors, or if you're asked to pay a high percentage of your debt as a settlement, you could end up spending more than you anticipated.

Debt settlement payments themselves can be moderately costly as well. While settling the debt does reduce the amount you owe, it may not reduce it nearly as much as you think. Debt settlements in the U.S. might range from 10% to 50% of what is due. Getting your debt cut down by 90% to only 10% of your previous owed amount is phenomenal, as decreasing it by merely 50% might not entirely be what you were anticipating. In this way, debt settlement can still be costly, even though most people still end up paying less than they would without making any changes.

Debt settlement may not always be a quick route to slashing your debts, but that doesn't mean it's worthless. As long as you know going into it that settlement can be costly in some circumstances; you can prepare for these costs and avoid getting hit with an unexpected bill. This will enable you to utilize debt settlement to its fullest extent as you proceed through the necessary steps.

## THE FIVE STEPS OF DEBT SETTLEMENT

The best way to avoid falling victim to the risks of debt settlement is to know the rules of the game, which will allow you to navigate the debt settlement process properly. First, before contacting any debt settlement companies, you can try to negotiate better rates on your loans and credit lines yourself. You could turn an unpayable loan into a manageable one if your lender is amenable to adjusting the terms, all without having to spend a cent on debt settlement and without putting a black mark on your credit. However, this may not be a viable option for you, either because your lender is unwilling to play ball or because even a lower monthly payment would still be impossible for you to keep up with. In these cases, proceeding with the debt settlement process is necessary and will likely net you the results you're looking for as long as you know the proper steps to take.

Debt settlement is a five-step process. It involves looking for the right company to work with, making a plan for carrying out the settlement, saving the necessary funds, negotiating, and finally, settling your debts. Once you have completed each of the five steps, you'll have a more manageable amount of debt that will allow you to work on improving your credit score freely.

**Step One: Find the Right Company**

You can technically go through the debt settlement process yourself. Still, in the vast majority of cases, you are better off paying for the services of a professional debt settlement organization. Suppose you opt to brave the field of debt settlement yourself without knowing all the ins and outs of working with lenders, how to negotiate effectively, and what forms you'll need to submit. In that case, you may overlook opportunities to save. You may get a less favorable settlement. You could waste time and energy arguing with lenders for months on end. You could even jeopardize your ability to get a debt settlement if you don't follow the proper channels. The risk becomes even greater if you have multiple debts you want to settle. In short, if you don't know what you're doing, debt settlement is a somewhat convoluted process, so it's best to entrust it to the professionals.

At the same time, not all companies that advertise their abilities to settle your debts are quite as good at it as they claim. Going with a low-quality organization that simply isn't a good fit can make it much harder to get the debt settlement you deserve. You'll want to research your choices carefully before selecting one. After all, it's your money—you should be wary about who you entrust it to.

Some companies operate under the guise of organizations that want to help you eliminate your debts and restore your credit, but they are just looking to take your money under the surface. These companies use unethical practices to scam you or lie to lenders to secure debt settlements. Predatory credit repair and debt settlement companies don't have your best interests at heart. Know what to look out for so you can separate the scams from the genuine debt settlement companies. Typically, if something sounds too good to be true, it probably is. Avoid companies that promise you the moon with debt settlement. Any organization that says it can wipe all your debt instantly is lying to you, as are those that say your credit report will be completely reset. No company can wipe away debt completely unless you file for bankruptcy, so any debt settlement company that suggests this is trying to con you.

Another red flag to look out for is companies that encourage you to declare false information. If your debt settlement company tells you to lie on a form or dispute parts of your payment history that you know is correct, this is your cue to get up and walk away. You don't want to involve yourself in credit fraud, which can have serious repercussions. Also, avoid making any payments before a company has rendered its services. Typical debt settlement companies will not charge you until they have gone through all the necessary steps to resolve your outstanding debt. The protocol for payments can vary from organization to organization, but it's typically not a good idea to give anyone money until they've begun the debt settlement process.

As a borrower and a customer of credit repair companies, you are protected by the Credit Repair Organizations Act (CROA). The most important part of the Act is that companies must make their costs known up-front, and they cannot charge surprise fees. They also cannot charge you anything before they have actually performed any services. Any organizations found to be in violation of ethical business practice standards can be fined or otherwise penalized. The Federal Trade Commission (FTC) may even opt to shut these organizations down. If you believe you may have been scammed, or if you notice any companies employing unethical practices, contact the FTC right away so they can launch an investigation.

Finding the right debt settlement company involves keeping an eye out for red flags and looking for high-quality companies that can help you get your finances in order. These companies should clearly explain the steps they will take to reduce your debt, as well as what you will owe for their services. Great debt settlement companies have an easy-to-read and understandable contract that estimates how long services will take. You may also want to work with companies that have been in operation for a few years at a minimum to reduce further the risk of being scammed. Additionally, make sure your debt settlement company of choice manages your kind of debt. Some companies can assist with medical debt, student loans, and medical bills, while others may focus on one or two types of debt. A simple search will tell you all you need to know about most companies, so take a few minutes to ensure everything is in order before picking the company that works best for you.

**Step Two: Plan and Budget**

Once you've found the right company for your needs, work with them to develop a strategy for debt settlement. You'll need to have a good idea of how much you can afford to pay in a lump sum to each lender that you owe. If you haven't been keeping a good record of your financial history and income versus expenses up to this point, start doing it now so that you can make an accurate estimate of your available funds.

If you don't already have one, a budget is a great place to start, whether you're preparing for debt settlement or you just want to work on getting your finances in order. Many people avoid budgeting because they feel like it's a waste of time since they know what they spend money on. In truth, it is often effortless to spend more money than you realize on unnecessary purchases, which means you're wasting money that you would be better off saving. Even if you don't typically buy luxuries, you can still benefit from knowing exactly where all of your money is going and how much you have left for saving or spending at the end of each month.

Your budget is composed of your income, your fixed expenses, and your variable expenses. Income is straightforward. It's all the money you make in a given period. Most budgets are calculated on a month-to-month basis, though you can also make a weekly or bimonthly budget if you like. Start by adding up all of your sources of income, including the money you make from work, side hustles you might have, and any other sources of cash you anticipate receiving within the month. If your income varies month over month, estimate on the lower end of what you usually bring home, so you won't be planning to spend money you might not have.

Once you've totaled your income, then write down all of your fixed expenses. Fixed expenses remain the same each month. They include insurance, rent, mortgage, and car payments, all of which cost the same amount from month to month.

By contrast, you also have variable expenses, which may be a bit more or less every month. Ordinary variable expenses include what you spend on clothing, food, entertainment, and gas. The amount of money you contribute to your savings is a variable expense. However, if you aren't making a dedicated effort to save, it may just be whatever is left of your income after all costs are taken out. Since you won't have an exact number for variable expenses, you'll have to estimate based on how much you have spent on them in the past. You can download my free budgeting tool by going to https://allenanything.com.

Once you've tallied up your income and expenses, you'll have a much clearer idea of where your money is going. You'll also be able to see what costs might be exceeding your expectations. Maybe you assumed most of your money was going to rent and food, but in reality, there were a lot of entertainment expenses you didn't notice before. Now that you have a budget, you can adjust the amounts to better align with the dollar amount you would like to be spending. Give yourself a limit for the amount you will pay each month on dining at restaurants and going to the movies, or anywhere else your spending might be a little overboard. If you're in a tight spot financially, you may want to save more than you would usually until you no longer deal with so much debt.

Now that you have your budget that serves as your financial plan, all you have to do is stick to it. As you make purchases throughout the month, write them down and deduct the amounts from your budget to see how quickly you approach your target spending amounts. If you're only halfway through the month and you've already nearly surpassed your budget for food, this indicates you may be making excessive purchases. Learning to curb your spending habits allows you to have greater control over your money, making it easier to save for a rainy day.

Sometimes, you will come up short of what you need to settle your debts. There's an excellent chance that the money you save from no longer paying down what you owe still might not be enough to cover the total cost of a settlement. In these circumstances, you'll want to devise a plan that allows you to save up more money before it's time to settle. In most cases, negotiations for debt settlement can take quite a while. Just because you don't have the funds now doesn't mean you can't raise them for a few months. To do so effectively, however, you will need to change the way you approach saving.

**Step Three: Focus on Savings**

At this point in the debt settlement process, you should have a good idea of how much money you need to save to settle your debts, assuming the lenders agree. Now you just need to bridge the gap between what you currently have on hand and what you need. This means focusing your efforts on saving money until you've reached your target.

One major mistake many people make in regards to saving is failing to prioritize it.

- Do you have a specific portion of your paycheck that you deposit into a savings account every month, or do you only save what is left after you have done all of your spending?
- Do you pay attention to how much is left over after expenses?
- Do you have a separate savings account or does all of your money go in and out of the same account?

Your answers to these questions can point towards very different levels of success with saving, as you may be unknowingly making the process harder for yourself.

Rather than simply saving whatever remains after you've spent the rest of your income, even if that amount is zero, start on the right foot by making sure always to contribute at least a given percentage or specific amount of your paycheck to your savings. Set a specific savings goal and ensure you meet that goal every month before worrying about buying nonessentials. It doesn't have to be a large percentage of your paycheck if you deal with many other expenses. It can be as small as just two to five percent, but even committing to this small amount will ensure you are continually growing your savings.

One great way to commit to saving if you have automated deposit paychecks is to have your company deposit part of every paycheck into a separate savings account. If you pay for everything out of a single checking account, it's easy to lose track of how much you're trying to keep on hand. The temptation to spend is made incredibly difficult to ignore, and it's unfortunately simple to go over budget without realizing it. With a separate savings account, you know how much you are allowing yourself to spend and how much you need to conserve, so you're not at risk of burning through the money you need to raise for your debt settlement.

There are many other methods you can use to make saving easier as well. For example, you could apply for refinancing on home and auto loans if the majority of your money is spent here and not enough is leftover to allow for savings. You may be able to lower other bills like phone, internet, and electricity by switching to a different provider, using them less often, or getting a cheaper package. You might miss out on a few TV channels or some extra data on your cell phone, but these inconveniences will be worth it for the money you'll gain back. Additionally, consider taking advantage of sales and discounts when you need to buy expensive items. Look for free or cheap entertainment options or clip coupons before you go to the grocery store. Plan your purchases out in advance so you can decide whether or not they fit into your budget while still allowing you to save your spare change. You can also attempt to limit impulse purchases by avoiding online shopping or just taking five minutes to consider the pros and cons of purchasing before pulling the trigger. These are all minor adjustments, but they add up over time, and can help you funnel money into your savings account on a more regular basis rather than accidentally draining your savings.

The best part about learning these methods for more effective saving practices is that they won't just help you during debt settlement. Continuing to prioritize saving money will help you for the rest of your life. It will vastly reduce the likelihood that you end up in severe debt again since you will be able to rely on your savings for emergency expenses. It will encourage you to be more mindful about your money and cut back on unnecessary spending. It will even help ensure you can enjoy a comfortable retirement later in your life. Take time now to revamp how you approach savings, and you will be reaping the rewards for years to come, long after you have settled all your current debts.

**Step Four: Engage in Negotiations**

For the most part, debt settlement negotiations will occur between your lender and the company you've chosen to handle the settlement details. Still, whether you decide to go hands-off or if you're pursuing settlement by yourself, it's a good idea to familiarize yourself with the basics of the process. Negotiating can be tricky because the offers you get will depend on many factors like your lender, your current financial situation, negotiation skills, and your debt settlement company of choice. Learning a little more about negotiations means you can be sure you are getting the best possible deal for your circumstances, and you can push for a better deal if one is available.

First, try to set realistic expectations. Reductions in debt differ significantly. While some people can reduce their debt by as much as 90 percent, it's infrequent. Others may only qualify for about a 40 percent reduction or somewhere in between these two numbers. If you go into debt settlement thinking you will only have to pay 10 percent of what you owe and get off scot-free, you'll likely be in for a rude awakening. At the same time, you don't want to accept a deal that is too low. You may not be able to waive 70 percent of your debt if it's your opening offer, but if your lender doesn't budge on waiving less than 40-50 percent, taking this deal may not help you much at all. If negotiations go awry, consider letting the debt go unpaid for a few more months and continuing to feed your savings. This will most certainly hit your credit score harder, but it will also make your lender more likely to accept better debt settlement terms.

In general, the more money you have saved up for settlement, the better of a deal you can get. A lender is more likely to take an upfront payment of $5,000 than settle for $3,000 or $2,000 on the same debt. Still, individual lenders may be more or less likely to offer significant debt reduction, so your mileage may vary. Lenders may also be less willing to negotiate a favorable settlement if you don't seem to be in too difficult of a financial situation. If you've been consistently keeping up with your minimum payments, there's little reason for your lender to believe you will no longer be able to do so. Therefore, you should only attempt settlement with debts that have gone unpaid for multiple billing periods or you're unlikely to get a favorable settlement.

One helpful tip is approaching negotiations with a straightforward story and not deviating from it or adding unnecessary details. You want to make it clear you're in a tough spot financially, but you don't need a sob story that spans half an hour to accomplish this, nor does it reflect well on you if you are constantly coming up with new reasons why you need to settle your debts. Tell the lender why you no longer have the available funds to pay what you owe, as well as what you plan to do if you cannot reach a settlement, such as filing for bankruptcy. Ideally, this should be a truthful story, ensuring there's less risk of mixing up your details and getting caught in a lie. Remain personable and friendly as well. Shouting at the person on the other end of the phone is unlikely to get you a better deal, and they'll be less inclined to feel sympathetic toward you, which can quickly turn the tides of any negotiation.

Whether you are doing the negotiations yourself or going through a debt settlement service, make sure to get the terms of the agreement in writing when everything is finalized. You should keep a paper copy of the settlement details for your records, which will prevent the lender from pursuing the debt or passing it along to a collections agency, thereby violating the agreement. Keeping a journal lets you defend yourself against any false claims, and it allows you to quickly correct any errors which might reflect on your credit report in the future.

**Step Five: Debts Settled!**

Once negotiations are over, you have everything in writing, and you've made the appropriate payments to your lender to settle your debts, you can breathe a sigh of relief knowing you are free of the burden you previously carried. Debt can cause a lot of stress, so take a moment to celebrate and relax. Successfully settling your debts is a great feeling—just be sure not to celebrate so thoroughly that you end up getting yourself right back into debt.

The truth of the matter is even though you may have paid off some of your debts, you may not have reached the end of the road just yet. For one, you may still need to settle or pay down other debts. So you are starting the process over again, including saving up money, which can take some time. Luckily, it will be easier to save now that you have fewer debts to worry about, which typically makes settling multiple debts a little easier. Another complication comes from the fact that even if you don't owe any money, this doesn't necessarily mean your credit has improved. On the contrary, debt settlement is scored negatively, and there's a good chance your lenders will close your credit lines once you settle your debts. So while the end of the debt settlement process can be a time for celebration, it's also an opportunity to review your credit and start taking the proper steps toward credit repair.

## EFFECTS ON YOUR CREDIT

In the short term, debt settlements do your credit score no favors. In addition to the negative impact of missing payments prior to settling the debt, any debt on your report that is marked as 'settled' will carry with it a hefty penalty on your score. After all, lenders want to know they can trust you to pay them back. Settling your debts implies that you aren't financially soluble enough to do so, at least for the time being. Settled debts remain on your report for seven years or longer. And depending on the specific circumstances, they can drop your credit score by as much as 100 points. This effect is nothing to scoff at, and it's one of the many reasons why debt settlement shouldn't be your first choice when you're looking to improve your credit score.

Still, needing to settle your debts doesn't condemn you to have a lousy score forever. Even with a 100-point hit to your score, you can still bring it up to a respectable 600-700 if you are diligent about adopting better saving and borrowing habits in the future. It will take some time, but the long-term impact on your score can be positive if you use debt settlement as an opportunity to change the way you use credit. Though it's not a pretty blank slate, minimizing your debts means you can save more money rather than spending it all on your monthly statements. This, in turn, means that when you get a new credit card, purchase only what you can afford to pay off within the month, so you won't run the risk of letting your debts pile up again in the future. Having money in your savings account also means that an unexpected emergency won't completely wipe you out, so you're far more likely to be able to restore your credit as time goes on.

Keep in mind that having a lower score due to settling your debts can make it more difficult for you to qualify for credit lines and loans in the future. Rebuilding your credit can be tricky and time-consuming, with your best efforts frustrated by lenders who don't trust you to make responsible decisions with credit. You may have an easier time qualifying for cards targeted toward younger people getting their first credit cards since these tend to accept applicants with minimal credit history. Look for cards that have no annual fees, and if there is a high interest rate, be sure to make all payments on time, so you don't have to pay any interest. After a few months of making exclusively on-time payments, you should have little trouble qualifying for a better card as your credit steadily improves.

## SENDING LETTERS TO CREDITORS

If you're planning on handling the debt settlement process yourself, you'll need to contact lenders through the appropriate methods. While discussions of debt settlement can begin on the phone, it's a bad idea to make all negotiations this way. Just because a lender agrees to something verbally doesn't mean they will be faithful to their word. Additionally, verbal agreements tend to fall through the cracks in large companies, and the details get forgotten. You don't want to be left with no recourse if you and the lender are both claiming you agreed to different settlement terms, so your safest bet is to send letters and hold onto all correspondence between you and your lenders.

You will likely need to exchange multiple letters with your lenders throughout the debt settlement process, especially during negotiations. If you're inexperienced with debt settlement, it's hard to know what to document. Avoid revealing your inexperience by using debt settlement letter templates and including all relevant information on both your initial offer and counteroffer.

**Beginning Negotiations**

Writing a debt settlement letter is a bit like writing a cover letter for a job application. It would help if you made sure you concisely hit all relevant points. You also need to present yourself a sure way to get your letter taken seriously. For a job, you want to list the reasons why you would be well-suited to the role. For debt settlement, you want to explain to a lender why you cannot pay what you owe and why debt settlement is a good option for both of you. In both situations, you aim to beat out the 'competition,' whether it is a fellow job applicant or a collections agency.

Start your letter off with the appropriate contact information. Include your name, address, phone number, and the name and address of the company you're sending the letter to. Be sure to jot down the date as well for your record keeping. Finally, include the relevant account number so your lender can easily find the debt you're requesting to settle.

Be clear about why you are writing and what you want. A debt settlement letter doesn't need to be longer than two or three paragraphs. Start out by saying you want to settle your debt for the account listed above, and you also want to remove late payments related to the account from your credit report. Then explain why you can no longer keep up with payments. Again, honesty is a good policy here, especially since the lender may want to verify your claims. If you say you were laid off from your job, they might check with your employer if you worked for a large company. They may request a doctor's note if you claim you were injured. You certainly won't be able to get away with a lie involving a natural disaster, and you don't want to be caught telling tall tales, so keep it simple and truthful.

Once you've covered the problem, move toward the solution. Make your initial offer for how much you will pay in exchange for settling the debt. A good starting offer is about 30 percent of what you owe, depending on what you can afford to pay. You aren't likely to get away with paying just a third of your debt, but this gives you a good starting point from which to make counteroffers. Finish your letter with a request for a signed written agreement containing a promise to pay in the offered amount and a requested response deadline.

Before sending the letter, make a copy and save it for your records. Create a specific folder for all copies of debt negotiation correspondence. This ensures you will not lose track of them or accidentally throw them away. You may also want to consider sending the letter by certified mail, so there is a record of when the lender received your letter and when they responded. This helps you avoid any disputes involving claims that the company never received your letter or that you took too long to respond.

Once you've mailed your letter, simply wait for the lender's counteroffer. This can take a few weeks, but there is no maximum time limit. If you don't receive a response within a month, you may need to consider other methods for pursuing settlement, like paying a company to perform the negotiations for you. Ideally, though, you will get a counteroffer not too long after you contact your lender. At this point, negotiations begin in earnest.

## Responding to a Counteroffer

In nearly all cases, lenders will not be willing to accept your initial proposal. Instead, they will respond to your offer with an offer of their own. Chances are, the amount they request you pay will be higher than what your budget allows for, so you will need to engage in negotiations until you've brought the payment down to something more manageable. Lenders expect you to negotiate the settlement terms with them, so don't feel like you aren't allowed to request more favorable terms. Still, you and the lender are at odds in this situation, so you'll need to be clear about why the proposed amount doesn't work for you.

In your counteroffer letter, explain why you cannot afford the amount they have requested. Again, be clear and concise when talking about your situation. You can mention that you have multiple debts to settle and only so much money available. A lender may be more inclined to accept your offer if they feel that waiting too long means you won't be able to pay your debt back at all. Be sure to include your counteroffer as well, so it falls between your initial offer and your lender's proposed settlement.

Negotiations can be daunting with the back and forth. They may persist for some time depending on what you are willing and able to pay and how your lender responds. If you are ready to pay a higher settlement, you may be able to end negotiations quickly. If you want to get the best possible payment reduction, you'll likely need to engage in negotiations for a while longer. Eventually, your lender may decide to agree to your conditions to prevent communications from dragging out any longer, which could be costing them more money in staffing than it's worth. In other cases, your lender may refuse to negotiate a settlement altogether. While unfortunate, it's always a risk to keep in mind with debt settlement. If you cannot reach an agreement, you'll be stuck with the debt and any added late fees that accrued during the negotiations. The good news is that by now, you should have saved up enough money in preparation for the settlement that you can afford to make payments for a while as you consider your next move.

### Dealing With Creditors Versus Collectors

Your best bet when settling debts is to speak directly to the company that first issued you a loan or line of credit. You are more likely to get a favorable deal from a creditor than a collector because they have more to lose. Your creditor doesn't want to spend time, money, and other resources tracking you down and getting you to pay what you owe, and they don't want to lose money selling your debt to a collector for a fraction of what it's worth. However, if you wait too long to start the negotiation process, you may be stuck dealing with a collection agency instead. Collectors are typically less receptive to debt settlement offers because their whole business is tracking down people who owe money and getting them to pay. They want to make as much money on the debt they bought as possible; otherwise, they risk losing money on their purchase. Worse, they have all the resources they need to continuously hound you for the money, which means they may not be willing to accept a lower offer that an original creditor might agree to.

When you're negotiating your debts with collectors, you'll need to approach the situation in a slightly different way. First, even before negotiations begin, you'll likely want to save more money since you will need to offer more to make the debt settlement attractive. Additionally, ensure you're sending your debt settlement letters to the right place. You don't want to go through all the trouble of sending out a letter to the original creditor or a previous collections agency only to find out the debt has changed hands. This puts you in an even more disadvantageous position by waiting longer to send the debt settlement request. Make sure you know who is trying to collect on your debt right now, including their company name and address, and don't offer to pay any companies that have already sold your debt to someone else.

Finally, while many people tend to ignore contact from debt collectors, this may not be the best move for you if you're planning to settle. At the very least, read all communications carefully, and save them rather than shredding them. You want to know what the collections agency has already offered you and how much money they are demanding. In some cases, they may ask for more than what the debt is worth, or they may violate regulations regarding what collectors are and aren't allowed to do. For example, a debt collector may not continue trying to contact you once they've received a written request from you to cease contact. An exception might be to inform you they have received your request and subsequently notify you of any other actions that may be taken against you, such as lawsuits. However, keep in mind that the debt does not disappear, and if you are looking to settle, you are likely going to want to keep this line of communication open. Still, take note of any efforts to contact and harass you outside of what is allowed, as pointing out these infractions can give you a leg to stand on during negotiations.

However, you choose to contact your creditors, always be mindful of the short-term and long-term impacts of debt settlement on your credit score. Even a successful settlement can still make it challenging to repair your credit without some serious work on your end. If you feel debt settlement isn't the right path for you or want to take further action to improve your credit score, other options like credit repair services may be better suited to your needs.

# 4

# CREDIT REPAIR

*"You cannot fix what you will not face."*

— JAMES BALDWIN

Despite thousands of people having incorrect information on their credit reports, very few people make an effort to correct this information, even when it is holding them back from qualifying for the loans and lines of credit they apply for. This isn't due to simple laziness, but because most people don't know these issues exist. They don't check their credit reports regularly or request a copy of their report from only one of the major bureaus rather than all three. They skim without trying to verify or scrutinize any of the information that closely. They trust that all accounts are reported accurately. In practice, many people have errors hiding in their credit reports that they don't know about.

If you haven't reviewed your credit reports recently, there's a chance you could be in the same position. It would help if you corrected any errors on your credit reports as soon as possible. It is the simplest, fastest, and cheapest way to raise your credit score with minimal effort on your part. If your score is low because of outstanding debts, you'll have to pay them down. If your score suffers from a spotty history of making payments on time, it could take years before the adverse effects of these missed payments are outweighed by on-time ones. If, on the other hand, your score is only artificially low due to incorrect or unverified information, you don't have to do much more than call these errors to attention to have them expunged from your record. This is what credit repair services are created to do.

Credit repair companies, like the Financial ER (https://thefinancialer.com), will look at your credit reports from each of the three major bureaus and identify any information that may be disputable. Everything from late payments to accounts that may have been mistakenly reported under your name. Other disreputable credit repair companies may promise to do so, but these services aren't able to remove genuine negative marks against your credit from your reports. If you did miss a payment, this demerit against you would remain. However, if any of these faulty items are misreported or cannot be verified by the lender, a credit repair service will work to have them removed from your report, so they no longer impact your score.

While credit repair itself is integral if mistakes affect your credit score, credit repair services can be hit or miss. Some companies try to subvert the rules and remove genuine items. Others operate above-board, but they still charge expensive fees that may not be worth the time you save from not performing the same steps yourself. Get to know the pros and cons of using a credit repair company so you can decide if it's a good fit for you or how to perform the same credit repair tactics on your own.

## WHY CREDIT REPAIR IS IMPORTANT

If you have less than stellar credit, you likely have many negative marks that lower your score. Missed payments harm your score, and if you go too long without making a payment on an account, this minor penalty can turn into a more significant charge-off. If you failed to pay your taxes one year, the federal government could impose a tax lien on your property, ensuring they receive the proceeds if you choose to sell assets like your home or car. It may not seem like it, but tax liens can also negatively affect your credit score. If you had to file for bankruptcy in the past, this would also show up on your credit reports.

Your credit reports are meant to reflect an accurate history of your credit usage. Still, since most lenders are large companies that handle thousands of customers, and the bureaus that compile your information into credit reports are even more significant, it's not uncommon for mistakes to occur. If you have a late payment, tax lien, charge-off, or bankruptcy under your name that shouldn't be there, it can significantly lower your score, all because of a mistake you might not have otherwise caught if you weren't keeping an eye on your credit reports.

Credit repair companies assist with the process of correcting these mistakes, so they don't harm your credit any longer. They contact creditors to negotiate and dispute charges that should not be on your report. They also request verification for any negative marks against you. If the creditor has no record of the debt, it likely was mistakenly applied to your account, and you can get these removed as well. Credit repair is a genuinely important service because there is no reason you should have to pay for a mistake someone else made. There are very few drawbacks in engaging in credit repair other than the cost if you choose to pay for professional help, so you can easily combine it with other cheap or free methods for improving your credit, like credit counseling. At the same time, on its own, credit repair can only help you in the short term, and it cannot help much if everything on your report is accurate. If you want to make a lasting positive change in your credit score, you must use credit more responsibly in the future, and you must also avoid credit repair scams that only exist to take your money.

**Protecting Yourself Against Fraud**

Like with debt settlement companies, many credit repair organizations aren't as helpful as they seem, so it's essential to look into any company before you decide to pay for their services. The CROA offers consumer protections here as well. According to the act, a credit repair company cannot tell you to lie to a credit bureau to get an unfavorable account removed from your report. They cannot charge you for services they didn't perform or advertise any guarantee that they can remove certain information from your report. While credit repair is advantageous if there are mistakes on your accounts, there is no guarantee that the bureaus will remove these mistakes, so avoid any companies that make these kinds of promises. If you feel a credit repair agency has defrauded you, you can sue the company for damages.

Perform a background check before you entrust your credit health to any company. Look into accounts from people who have worked with the company before and see whether they advertise reasonable services or make unrealistic guarantees. Of course, the best way to ensure a credit repair company doesn't defraud you is to review your credit yourself, though this comes with its own drawbacks. Scanning your credit reports for errors takes time and energy, and disputing the errors involves contacting the relevant companies and filing disputes. This can be intimidating for many people without prior experience, which is why they turn to credit repair agencies, but it isn't impossible if you know what steps to take.

## THE FIVE STEPS OF CREDIT REPAIR

Repairing your credit yourself rather than paying for a company's services is a perfectly viable option for most people. Executing credit repair tactics regularly is a great way to ensure there aren't some mistakes on your credit report that are harming your score unbeknownst to you. Since credit repair costs nothing when you do it yourself, other than a few hours of your time, it's a good idea to review your credit reports from each of the major bureaus once a year when you request your annual free copy of your credit reports.

**Step One: Get a Copy of Your Credit Report**

You're going to have a tough time reviewing your credit if you have no idea what the three major bureaus have been reporting. Even if you know your credit score, you may not see every factor determining whether you have good or bad credit. Therefore, the first step in any credit repair strategy is to get an updated copy of your credit report. Remember that you will have to get a copy from each of the three major credit bureaus and that you can request a copy of your information from TransUnion, Equifax, and Experian once a year without paying a fee or penalizing your credit score. If you do not want to contact the bureaus directly, you can also get your reports from sites like annualcreditreport.com, as mentioned in Chapter 1.

If you have already requested a copy of your credit report within the year, you can use it for credit repair, but keep in mind that it may not be fully up to date if it has been a while. Make sure to file your credit report in a secure location to avoid it being lost or damaged. Should you misplace or shred it before you decide to pursue credit repair, you'll need to pay for a new copy.

Alternatively, you could wait out the year until you can get a new one for free, but this isn't recommended as it allows errors to remain on your report and lower your score for additional months. It's best to act as soon as possible with credit repair, as the quicker you can get these mistakes removed from your report, the swifter your credit score will improve.

**Step Two: Review for Errors**

Now that you have your reports, the next step is to review them for errors. Start by checking for any accounts you don't recognize or any missed payments you don't remember making. Double-check that all of your personal information is correct, including your full name, address, birth date, and social security number. If any of this information is incorrect, you'll want to contact the relevant bureau right away to get it fixed.

Look out for red flags on your credit report, such as discrepancies between information from different bureaus. In some cases, this isn't an issue and only reflects that many creditors report accounts to just one or two of the three bureaus. In other cases, however, it could mean the information is incorrect on one of the reports. If you notice any discrepancies, principally if these harms your credit score, try to verify them with your records. If you can't remember missing a payment or taking out a loan that only appears on one report and don't have any records of doing these things, you will need to dispute the negative mark.

**Step Three: Dispute Discrepancies**

Once you've compiled a list of potential errors and discrepancies between your credit reports, you're ready to start correcting them. You'll need to dispute each incorrect item with the appropriate bureau. Just like with debt settlement, it's best to have everything in writing, so send your dispute in the form of a letter and make a copy for your records. You do not have to pay a fee to dispute a discrepancy on your report, but you should avoid sending excessive and unnecessary disputes for valid items. Once the bureau receives your notice, they will perform their own investigation, typically taking about a month. Keep copies of all correspondence between yourself and the bureau until the issue is resolved.

Disputing discrepancies is the trickiest part of the credit repair process and if you have never done it before, you may be unsure of how to start. See Chapter 7 for a how-to guide that goes through the steps of submitting a dispute and successfully removing a faulty item from your credit report.

**Step Four: Always Pay Valid Debts on Time**

Filing disputes is a fantastic first step for raising your credit score, but your efforts shouldn't stop there. Even if you remove every mistaken demerit against you, you likely have real negative marks that bring your score down, and there is no fast and easy method for removing these. Instead, you must outweigh them with consistent on-time payment of any outstanding debts.

Note that if you believe a debt on your report isn't valid and you dispute it, there's no need to pay it down, as doing so won't help your credit score once the mistake is corrected. Focus your efforts on paying off any valid debts you still have, which means keeping up with regular payments. The best way to consistently raise your score is to make many on-time payments in a row, as this demonstrates to lenders that you are responsible with your money. Just making a payment each month can make a world of difference for your credit score, as I covered in my other book, *Make a Payment*.

You cannot avoid debt by ignoring it; you will only make it worse the longer you go without making payments. As you continue to miss payments, your credit score will plummet, and there's nothing you can do to remove valid debts from your credit report. To prevent your debts from becoming more significant problems in the future, pay them down now, or use strategies like debt consolidation to make the process more feasible if you can't keep up with your current payments. Get into the habit of staying on top of your debts, so you can develop a healthier relationship with the way you use credit.

**Step Five: Lower Your Credit Utilization**

One of the most significant factors contributing to debt and, as a result, a poor credit score is high credit utilization. Your credit utilization measures how much credit you're currently using compared to how much you have available. If you're using half of your available credit, you would have a credit utilization rate of 50 percent, regardless of how many credit cards you have under your name. If you have multiple credit cards maxed out or nearly maxed, your credit utilization is high. If you use just a tiny fraction of your available credit and pay it off on time each month, your credit utilization is low.

As you might expect, low credit utilization is favored in credit score calculations. Having a high outstanding balance typically means you cannot pay the balance in full at the end of each billing period. This means accrued interest and if you cannot make a payment on time or at all, additional fees. In addition to increasing your debt, high credit utilization harms your credit score so you don't want to let these issues linger.

According to Experian, credit utilization accounts for approximately 30% of what calculates your FICO score, which means improper utilization can tank an otherwise excellent or fair score.

One method for improving your credit utilization ratio is to open a new line of credit. Let's say that between all of your current credit cards, your total available credit is $10,000, and you currently owe $4,000. In this example, credit utilization is 40 percent. If you opened a new card with a credit limit of $2,000, you would then only be using a third of your available credit. In theory, this sounds like a quick and easy way to resolve utilization issues, but it isn't always a good strategy in practice. Consider whether having more credit available would tempt you to spend more. If you're likely to put a balance on the new card right away, you won't improve your credit utilization ratio much at all. Max out the new card, and you could be in an even worse spot than before. At the same time, you don't necessarily want to close cards either. Closing a card with a zero balance means the credit line is removed from your total available credit. Using the previous example again, let's say that instead of opening a new card, you close a line that had a $2,000 credit limit. Assuming your balance on all your cards remains the same, you would then be using 50 percent of your available credit, which could seriously harm your score.

If you want to reduce your credit utilization without opening or closing any accounts:

1. Work on paying down your debts.
2. Start by paying down the cards that are closest to being maxed out.
3. Pay balances with high-interest rates to keep your total amount owed as low as possible.
4. Remember that loan balances are left out of credit utilization calculations, so while you shouldn't let yourself fall behind on payments, you'll want to prioritize credit cards and similar lines of revolving credit.
5. Capitalize on the benefits of credit repair by chaining it together with paying off your debts.

Keeping your credit utilization low ensures you will have an easier time keeping up with your debt in the future, making credit restoration firmly within your grasp.

## THE 15/3 RULE

Repairing your credit means keeping up with card payments, but this can be difficult even with the best of intentions. Often, you may find that you just don't have enough money in the bank when your payment is due to pay it off in full. However, repeatedly making partial payments damages your credit and leads to further issues with your credit score later down the line.

One method that can make managing payments a little easier is following the 15/3 rule. Essentially, instead of paying your bill in full in one day, you split the amount in half and make two smaller payments a few days apart. The first payment is made 15 days before the due date, and the second is made three days before. While you end up paying the same amount of money, many people find that the 15/3 method makes it easier for them to keep up with their bills since they aren't making such a large payment at one time. Not only does this rule make it less likely for you to miss payments, it also has the potential to benefit your score even more than usual.

When you pay according to the 15/3 rule, you make two payments for every one billing period. This bimonthly approach is counted as two separate payments by most creditors. Now, instead of just making one on-time payment each month, you're making two. These two payments can translate to two positive marks on your credit report, which can outweigh any remaining negative impacts from missed and late payments. Note that this result isn't always guaranteed, depending on the way your creditor processes your payments. Still, the benefits are good enough to give it a shot, and there are effectively no risks associated with this method as long as you remember to make both payments.

Making bimonthly payments makes it easier for you to keep up with your bills, which grants you improved financial discipline. It also helps you reduce your credit utilization and debt-to-income ratio faster than with a traditional payment structure. Your debt decreases more rapidly, and the positive change is reflected in your account sooner. Perhaps the most significant factor is how the 15/3 method lets you save some money on interest for any loans and credit card lines you cannot pay in full.

If you follow the typical payment schedule, assuming you're on a monthly billing cycle, you make 12 payments per year. With the 15/3 method, the first payment you make in December is still considered part of the same year, whereas paying right before the due date would generally count for January of the new year. By using a bi-monthly payment strategy, you end up making 13 total monthly payments in a given year; putting an extra payment toward your debt each year means lower interest and faster repayment of debts. In short, the 15/3 method lets you turn regular debt repayment into a tool to quickly boost your credit score, as long as you are using the statement date and due date difference to your advantage.

**Statement Date Versus Due Date**

To fully use the 15/3 method, you must understand the difference between the statement date and the due date of a given credit card bill. The statement date, also known as the statement closing date, is the day you first receive a summary of your account and the amount you are required to pay. You don't need to pay off your bill the second you get your statement. Instead, you have a window of time here known as the grace period, where you won't be charged any interest on your card as long as you pay off the balance before the due date. The due date is the last possible day for you to make a payment without penalties or late fees. It typically occurs at least 21 days after you get your statement.

During this 21-day timespan, you can split up your payment without accruing additional interest. If you time it right, you can significantly reduce your credit utilization by making another purchase and paying it off right away. When you get your statement, check the due date and count back 15 days. This is the day you want to pay your balance. In a standard 15/3 method, you would pay half of your statement then and half 12 days later. However, if you absolutely want to maximize your gains from this strategy, pay off your entire bill 15 days before it is due. Then, once your statement is paid, make another minor purchase that doesn't use up much of your credit utilization. Make sure you can afford to pay for this purchase as well, so pick something reasonably inexpensive. Finally, three days before the due date, make that second payment, paying off the new minimal purchase. When your credit score is calculated, not only will you have made two on-time payments, but your credit utilization is significantly low for the second payment. Since your credit score is calculated with the most recent information available, you should have no issues keeping your credit utilization as low as possible using this method, which immediately impacts your score in a positive manner.

At the end of the day, there is no real way to 'cheat' your credit score. Missing payments and racking up significant amounts of debt will make it harder to maintain a good score and raise your score when it dips. Still, when you understand how your score is calculated and take the time to review your credit report for inaccuracies, you can eliminate many of the penalties that would otherwise harm your score. Credit repair can be advantageous if you know how to get the most out of it.

# 5

# THE FCRA AND KNOWING YOUR RIGHTS

*"Sharing experience and building public support for the full range of rights is more powerful than legal cases."*

— MARY ROBINSON

As a consumer, you have certain rights that protect you from predatory and unfair credit reporting practices. Credit bureaus and other companies involved in the credit reporting process have an obligation to take your concerns seriously when you believe you have been defrauded or when there is incorrect information on your credit report. As outlined in the Fair Credit Reporting Act (FCRA), these rights ensure that credit bureaus cannot take advantage of you, nor can they utilize any shady practices to make your score lower than it should be based on your actions as a borrower.

While the FCRA offers many protections, these protections are all but useless if you don't know what they are. You cannot stand up for your rights if you aren't aware that you have rights in the first place. Developing a better understanding of the FCRA will help you better navigate the uncertain waters of repairing your credit. Luckily, you don't have to understand all of the technical and legal terms in the Act to benefit from it. It would be best if you simply had a basic understanding of what the law allows you to do, what it will enable creditors and bureaus to do, and what it shields you from. Equip yourself with this knowledge so you can stand up for your rights and pursue the best credit repair strategy.

## BASICS OF THE FCRA

The FCRA was created primarily as a way to protect the confidentiality of borrowers' information. Your credit report is meant to be a comprehensive historical record of your debts; data has to change hands many times and from many different companies. Lenders supply loan and credit line details to bureaus and provide them with an ongoing summary of your payment history. Debt collectors pass along information about which debts are paid and which debts are not. Every time you apply for a new line of credit or loan, the company processing your request exchanges information with the credit bureaus. The whole system involves multiple parties, with plenty of opportunities for the wrong information to fall into the wrong hands.

The FCRA prevents companies and individuals from making unusual and unnecessary inquiries into your personal information. If you apply for a mortgage, you want the mortgage company to check your score, but you don't want them to have open access to that information forever. Rather than allowing just anyone to pull your credit records at any time for any reason, accessibility is strictly limited to entities upon a 'permissible purpose,' like creditors, landlords, and insurance companies. This includes potential employers during the hiring process in some states, though your written consent is requisite.

The FCRA also ensures you're notified about how information in your credit report is used. If you apply for credit or something else that involves a credit check, such as a job or an insurance policy, you have the right to know if you were denied based on your credit history. You can also request a file disclosure, which lets you see what credit information a given company has access to. You can opt-out of the pre-screened offers you get in the mail, and you have the right to freeze access to your account temporarily. Other protections exist to ensure you can dispute any incorrect information on your credit report and that a successful dispute means the information will be removed.

Given the number of protections the FCRA affords to all borrowers, it's almost hard to believe that the law only dates back to 1970, prior to which many of these provisions were not guaranteed. Consumers were at a much higher risk of having their information misused, and it was harder to understand who was accessing your credit report and why. Now, the FCRA serves as an essential law that protects you from fraud and keeps you in the loop about your credit score, specifically regarding the rights guaranteed by section 609.

## SECTION 609

Section 609 of the FCRA deals with your right to know your credit information. Just as companies can check your credit score and report in certain circumstances, you too can have access to this information, though thanks to the FCRA, you don't have to jump through quite so many hoops. Upon your request, all bureaus must disclose the information they have collected about you, typically in the form of your credit report. This is ideal, not just because you always have access to information about your score, since it allows you to identify and dispute false information during credit repair.

In addition to getting full disclosure about who has your information, section 609 also includes provisions about credit score disclosures. According to the FCRA, a creditor must also disclose your credit score, the possible score range, the report generation date, and any factors used in calculating the score. In other words, you have a right to know what your score is, how recently it was calculated, and how it was derived from various factors, including payment history and credit utilization. Without this information, improving your score would be much more challenging because you would be unaware of the most important factors to manage. Having full access to all relevant information about your credit score gives you the power to repair your credit since you can identify and dispute any false details, which is your right as guaranteed by the FCRA.

**Mistakes to Avoid**

While Section 609 affirms many of your rights as a consumer, people are frequently misinterpreting it by their eagerness to repair their credit as quickly as possible. Many credit repair services mention a "609 dispute letter," also known as a consumer disclosure, which is a specific template used in credit repair disputes. It is often regarded to be a foolproof plan for improving your credit. Supposedly, the 609 dispute letter is capable of removing even legitimate demerits from your credit report through a loophole of sorts. These companies claim that if you dispute a demerit by requesting validating documents, such as bankruptcy and loan agreement paperwork, the credit bureau won't be able to supply this information since they aren't the original lender. Therefore, they will be forced to remove the item from your report.

In practice, however, the 609 dispute letter isn't nearly as effective as the above stated claim. In actuality, the right to dispute incorrect items isn't guaranteed in Section 609 of the FCRA at all but rather in Section 611. For another, even Section 611 doesn't guarantee that unverifiable claims will be automatically removed from your credit report. When using a 609 letter requesting details a credit bureau doesn't possess, like original loan terms and statements, they're not required to provide you with those documents. Credit bureaus are only obligated to provide the information they have access to. Even if a bureau doesn't have original documents readily available, that doesn't automatically mean the item in your credit report is invalidated.

While the bureau must perform an investigation in response to all disputes, this just means the bureau will likely contact the creditor responsible for the account, who will verify the claim and end the investigation. Credit bureaus are only required to remove unverifiable or inaccurate information when disputing, if and only if they confirm the data is indeed incorrect. Missing a document or two about a loan does not constitute proving the information is false. You can and should use your ability to dispute wrong items responsibly, as you aren't likely to get very far by trying to utilize loopholes.

Another mistake people frequently make with disputes is placing too much value on the template used for the dispute letter. Many people are under the impression that using a particular template and wording your dispute a specific way will improve your chances of getting an item removed from your credit report. The truth is that not a single template serves as a magic bullet for poor credit. The bureau will perform the same investigation once you send a letter of dispute, regardless of the medium or the exact phrasing. Ensure that all pertinent information is accurately included so as avoid wasting your time and extending the credit repair process.

## SECTION 611

As mentioned above, it is Section 611, not Section 609, that covers your right to dispute incorrect information on your credit report. While many regulations minimize the frequency of errors on credit reports, mistakes happen, and things occasionally slip through the cracks. The FCRA guarantees that you can check for the presence of incorrect information on your credit reports from each of the major bureaus and that you can dispute these errors once you notice them.

In addition to affirming your right to dispute, Section 611 also ensures credit bureaus are obligated to respond to all inquiries, whether they come from large credit repair companies or individuals. This means you don't have to pay a costly fee to remove false information, and you can do it yourself if you follow the steps outlined in the previous chapter.

While Section 611 protects your right to dispute, be careful how you use this power. Don't dispute positive items if you're looking to improve your score because these cannot be re-added to your credit report once they are removed without proper verification. Since marks are removed if they are found to be unverified, this means there's little chance you will get back these points on your score if you dispute them. If you dispute a valid open account, your creditor may close the account assuming it was fraudulent; be sure to avoid this as well.

Also, avoid threatening to take legal action until you have exhausted your ability to dispute the items in question, and only do so when you have the proper grounds for it. If you have debts you couldn't pay and the marks against you are legitimate, do not dispute these either. You run the risk of getting sued if the account was closed recently enough depending on your state's laws, as it is considered fraud. In short, exercise your rights responsibly and only target truly incorrect items. If you follow these rules while taking advantage of the freedoms offered to you by the FCRA, you will avoid the worst mistakes people make when trying to repair their credit.

Of course, just because a Section 609 letter doesn't give you the ability to remove all unfavorable accounts with impunity, this doesn't mean there aren't any hidden methods for improving your credit. On the contrary, if you know what to look for, there are many methods you can use to improve your chances of having disputes settled in your favor as you work to repair your credit.

6

# THE SECRETS OF CREDIT REPAIR

Credit repair may seem simple on the surface, but as an outsider to the industry, there are many things you might not know about how lenders and bureaus operate. At times, these companies may withhold certain information from you if they believe they will benefit from it, even if it means you end up having to spend more of your time, energy, and money working to repair your credit.

Learning the trade secrets of the credit industry leaves you better prepared to navigate the process of credit repair and other methods for improving your credit, like debt settlement and credit counseling. Knowledge is power and discovering the closely-kept secrets of the companies that determine your credit score will better prepare you to advocate for your consumer rights while repairing your score.

## WHAT LENDERS DON'T WANT YOU TO KNOW

While the vast majority of lenders aren't actively looking to defraud you, this doesn't mean they always have your best interests at heart. After all, your goals differ significantly from those of your lender when a debt goes unpaid. Your lender wants to collect as much money as possible so they can turn a profit on the loan or credit line and you want to pay as little as possible to resolve the issue. Because of this, some lenders will pursue illegal strategies when attempting to collect on their debts. You can prevent this by developing a thorough understanding of the laws and regulations that protect you as a consumer, which will also help you take advantage of all avenues available to you for repairing your credit.

### The Fair Debt Collection Practices Act

Lenders, and by extension debt collectors, can only attempt to collect on unpaid debts in specific and regulated ways. The Fair Debt Collection Practices Act (FDCPA) prevents creditors from using deceptive lending practices, and it also restricts their ability to harass you when your debts go unpaid. The Act primarily applies to debt collection agencies, though it can also apply to collections departments affiliated with the original lender.

When a debt collector contacts you, they are required to provide basic information about the relevant account. This includes the collector company's name, where the debt was purchased, how much is owed, and a notice that you can dispute the debt if it does not belong to you or if it's already been paid. If you dispute a debt, it must be verified by the collector before they continue to request payment. This ensures you don't end up paying for a debt that cannot be verified and it can also be used to buy you some time to save up money if you cannot afford to pay off the debt right away.

The FDCPA also restricts how and when debt collectors are allowed to contact you. They cannot attempt to reach you at unusual or especially inconvenient times, and all calls and in-person visits must be between the hours of 8:00 am and 9:00 pm. They are not allowed to try to reach you at work if you cannot take the call without jeopardizing your job. They cannot persistently contact you in a harassing manner, nor can they make threats other than notifying you that they are pursuing a lawsuit. If you send the collection agency a letter requesting they no longer contact you, they can no longer do so legally, though the money you owe isn't erased, and they may still sue to attempt to collect the debt. If a lawyer represents you, they must direct all contact to your lawyer and cease contact with you once you have informed them of your legal representation. If a debt collector breaks any of these rules, keep a record of the infractions, as you may be able to sue.

Alongside the FDCPA, the Fair Credit Reporting Act (FCRA) places additional restrictions on how lenders can report your information to credit bureaus, including information about late and missed payments. The FCRA ensures that individuals can only access your credit report if they have a valid reason, so as to keep your information secure. Again, it is paramount to know your rights so you can fight back against any companies that request access to your credit information for fraudulent or deceptive purposes. Both the FCRA and the FDCPA afford you protections against lenders and collection agencies, so use them to your advantage to make the credit repair process as easy as possible.

**Questions Lenders Can't Ask**

You've likely heard that employers aren't allowed to ask you specific questions during a job interview, such as whether or not you have kids or if you own a car. This is because answering these questions a certain way could skew their decision-making process against you, and they may not offer you the job. What you might not know is that lenders are similarly restricted from asking you questions that are unassociated with the pending loan that may jeopardize your ability to qualify, even if your credit score would otherwise be high enough. You don't want all of your hard work improving your score to go to waste, so don't let lenders trip you up with these sneaky questions.

Lenders are allowed to ask basic questions that give them a better picture of how much risk they would be taking on by approving your request for a loan or credit line. However, they cannot ask invasive or irrelevant questions, nor can they lead you into disclosing this information about yourself. The Fair Housing Act makes it illegal for mortgage lenders to ask questions that discourage you from buying property in a given area. For example, "would you be okay buying a house in an area with a high crime rate?" Nor can they suggest you look elsewhere based on discriminatory factors such as your race, gender, or dependency on public assistance programs. These questions can result from attempted housing discrimination, so remember that you don't need to disclose any of this information when applying for credit.

Lenders also cannot ask questions about your eligibility to work. As long as you currently have an income that meets their threshold for credit approval, they cannot ask if you're pregnant or planning on taking time off from work to start a family, nor can they ask if you are disabled or ill. Similarly, while lenders will often ask about your marital status, they cannot reject you if they don't like your answer.

Even though lenders aren't allowed to ask certain questions, many do as they assume you aren't aware of your rights. Successfully qualifying for a new line of credit, which often means fielding some of these illegal questions, can make a big difference in your ability to raise your credit score. Know what questions you do and don't have to answer so you don't jeopardize your chances of loan approval as you work to repair your credit.

## WHAT THE BUREAUS DON'T WANT YOU TO KNOW

Ideally, the bureaus handling your credit should be as transparent as possible with their consumers. In practice, there are many items the bureaus may fail to inform you of, including how to easily dispute and investigate items on your credit report. Each investigation costs the bureaus time and money. A costly analysis is merely one reason why so many people don't even know they should regularly check their credit reports for errors. This is also why many people are too intimidated to perform credit repair themselves. The more you learn about the options available to you when you're struggling with your credit, the easier it is to bring your score up.

**Why Mixed Credit Profiles Occur**

From time to time, reporting errors will result in someone else's information ending up on your credit report, or vice versa. It is known as a mixed credit profile and when this occurs, it can seriously impact your credit. If someone else's credit mistakes are attributed to your credit report, it's your score that is penalized. If your on-time payment record is attributed to someone else, you'll miss out on the additional points you would otherwise gain on your credit score. Either way, this is a severe error, and yet it is surprisingly common.

In some cases, nearly one-third of consumer credit disputes are related to mixed credit profile claims. The obstacle is so significant that it once led to an $18-million lawsuit against one of the major credit bureaus, Equifax. But why is this issue so prevalent and what can you do about it?

One of the reasons why mixed credit profiles are so common is due to a lack of diligence by credit bureaus in confirming account information. Bureaus may use just seven of the nine digits in your social security number to attribute accounts to your name if they believe other information matches, which could lead to a grievous mix-up. If you have a common first and last name, there's a significant risk that your information could get mixed up with theirs if your social security numbers happen to be similar enough. This lack of care can also contribute to rising rates of identity fraud, which are often exacerbated by a lack of protections and checks when someone else opens an account in your name. What bureaus don't want you to know is that these kinds of issues are nothing new. As of 1990, the FTC brought this issue to the bureaus' attention, though little has been done since then to prevent mixed credit profiles from remaining a significant problem for thousands of borrowers. Knowing this information should encourage you to be more vigilant about checking your credit report so you can spot and dispute these errors as soon as they occur.

**Paying for Your Credit Score**

Credit bureaus can provide you with your credit score upon request, though the score comes with a small fee. You might assume that getting your score directly from the bureau ensures that you're getting the most accurate possible number, but this often isn't the case. Instead, bureaus will typically send, what is called, an 'educational score'—based on the individual's credit activity. This gives the consumer an idea of where they stand as borrowers as opposed to the actual score lenders see when reviewing loan applications. A false sense of how good or bad your credit is could affect your decision to apply for a given line of credit. If you apply with only an educational score in mind, you may get significantly different terms than anticipated. While it is true that there is no single score that every single lender uses, it's essential to know that paying to get your score from a credit bureau may not always be the best idea.

Luckily, there are plenty of ways for you to check your credit score without going through the bureaus and often without having to pay a cent. Many companies allow you to check your credit score from one or more of the bureaus as often as you like without fees or penalties to your score. Just make sure you select a reputable company; you don't want to put yourself at risk of identity theft.

**Optical Character Recognition (OCR)**

When sending a credit dispute letter, you probably assume that it is being received and read by a human being, but more often than not, this is untrue. Instead, credit bureaus make use of systems known as Optical Character Recognition (OCR) to field initial dispute letters. Since there is a tremendous volume of letters coming into these bureaus daily, letters are first screened by the OCR system, which attempts to separate valid claims from frivolous ones. The system accomplishes this by searching for keywords and phrases, meaning that if your dispute letter lacks these key features, the OCR system may discard your letter before a human ever looks at it.

Even if your letter makes it through OCR screening, it has to stand up to the e-OSCAR system, which performs an additional scan. The e-OSCAR system applies a code that labels your report as more or less likely to be legitimate. The result is that both algorithms may automatically reject dispute letters or slow down due to improper categorization.

One issue many people run into when they pay for a credit repair company's services is that the company is unaware of OCR and the e-OSCAR system. As a result, they flood credit bureaus with letters for frivolous disputes, making it far less likely that legitimate disputes will make it through the system. You can avoid this by handling the credit repair process yourself, as you're less likely to flag the system if you are only sending a few valid dispute letters with all relevant information included rather than a bunch of junk letters. Alternatively, you can work with an experienced credit repair service that understands OCR and e-OSCAR, as well as how to get through these systems. In either case, this is yet another reason why you should never just go with the first credit repair company you find and why you should always do your research before trusting someone with your credit.

## WHAT THE REPAIR AND SETTLEMENT COMPANIES DON'T WANT YOU TO KNOW

Repair and settlement companies claim to be on your side, but just like any other company, they are businesses looking to make money. Unfortunately, both fields are plagued with scams and con artists looking to turn a quick buck and are far less interested in helping you repair your credit. Many will promise you the moon as long as it convinces you to pay for their services, whether or not they can deliver on their promises.

Any company that offers repair and settlement services runs on the assumption that you don't know how to handle the process yourself. If you could settle debts and dispute credit report items on your own, you wouldn't need to pay someone else to do it, after all.

Therefore, the most significant factor these companies don't want you to know is that you can take matters into your own hands and save some money by doing everything yourself. It is far less complicated to repair your credit than many companies make it out to be and as long as you take the time to learn what you are doing, you likely don't need their help at all. Of course, just by reading this book, you are equipping yourself with the necessary knowledge for doing things on your own, so you know that it is not only possible, but ideal.

Still, not everyone is comfortable handling debt settlements and credit repair on their own. You may not have time to review your credit reports thoroughly, or you may not have the negotiation skills necessary for getting favorable settlements. If you decide that you are willing to pay for these services, always make sure you are going with a reputable company. Shop for prices, ask questions, and proceed with caution prior to paying for any services before they are rendered. A little extra caution can be an immense help in finding a debt repair or credit restoration service that knows what it is doing and isn't going to scam you. If you decide to take matters into your own hands, know that you have many tools at your disposal, including the one you may not already know about: pay for delete.

**Pay for Delete**

When you pay off an account, you generally no longer have any leverage with which to strike a deal with your lender. They have received their money, so they have no obligation to alter your payment records if you didn't already get them to agree to it in writing during settlement negotiations. The negative credit items left behind can continue to impact your score for up to seven years. However, if you have trade lines that harm your score and the associated accounts are still open, you have an opportunity to negotiate to have these accounts and all their adverse effects wiped off your credit report entirely.

Pay for delete is very similar to debt settlement, but in this case, you aren't negotiating just to close out a debt. You're also negotiating to effectively erase the record of your late and missed payments entirely. This will happen on its own eventually, but only after many years have passed, which can be a problem if you're looking to open a new line of credit to rebuild your score. The pay for delete method involves you and a lender or debt collector coming to an agreement before closing an account. Unlike with debt settlement, you must typically agree to pay the entire remaining balance, not just a fraction of it. However, if you are working with a third-party collections agency, you may be able to negotiate to pay more than what they purchased the debt for. In exchange, the collection agency agrees to remove all information associated with the debt from your credit report, including your record of missed payments.

While pay for delete may seem like an ideal strategy for getting negative items off your credit report sooner rather than later, it comes with complications that may make it a less than attractive option. For one, the FCRA frowns upon the pay-for-delete method, though it isn't explicitly banned. Under usual circumstances, any account that has been fully paid typically cannot be removed from your credit report and pay for delete subverts this. As a result, any records of the debt being settled exist in a legal gray area and they may not hold up if your lender or a collection agency attempts to take you to court over the debt in the future, though this outcome is rare. Additionally, once you pay a debt collection agency, they may not follow through and remove the account, especially if you don't have a record of the agreement.

In some cases, the pay-for-delete strategy can even be unnecessary due to changes in how your credit score is calculated. Paid collections accounts aren't included in your credit score with newer scoring models, so you wouldn't see an increase in your score even if the account was removed from your report. It would be best if you were especially wary of any credit repair service that utilizes pay-for-delete and makes false promises about its effectiveness. Carefully consider the benefits and potential downsides before pursuing the pay-for-delete strategy, just as you would with any other method of credit repair.

Improving your credit is often a lengthy process. While the tips and tricks discussed in this chapter can help speed things along, they aren't foolproof methods and they don't necessarily negate the fact that you will have to practice good borrowing habits to repair your credit truly. Combine your newfound insider information with responsible credit usage and dispute letters when they are appropriate, and you won't be steered wrong by lenders, bureaus, or credit repair companies.

7

# JUST DISPUTE IT

*"When a person realizes he has been deeply heard, his eyes moisten. I think in some real sense he is weeping for joy. It is as though he were saying, 'Thank God, somebody heard me. Someone knows what it's like to be me.'"*

— CARL ROGERS

In Chapter 4, you learned how the credit repair process works, including how powerful a tool such as dispute letters can be when used effectively. You should have a good idea of the basic steps involved in credit repair. These include requesting a copy of your credit report, reviewing it for any errors, filing disputes if you notice discrepancies, and improving your credit through paying down valid debts and lowering your credit utilization.

Now, we will look at the specific steps involved in writing and sending disputes if you want to remove inaccurate and unverifiable information from your credit report successfully. Dispute letters can be invaluable tools when used properly, but they won't help you much if you don't know how to write an effective one. Follow these important steps for disputing negative items on your credit report and you'll be one step closer to restoring your credit and regaining your financial freedom and independence.

## THE FIRST RULE OF CREDIT DISPUTES

Credit bureaus offer multiple methods for filing a dispute when you notice something unusual on your credit report. You can go online and go to the bureau's website in question, or you can write a physical letter and send it in the mail. The online method may be more convenient for you at the moment, but you will likely find that it isn't quite so fortunate in the long run and it can even halt the credit repair process in its tracks.

The first and most important rule of credit disputes is always sending your dispute letters by physical mail and not online. There are multiple reasons for this. For one, if you submit a dispute online, there is no easy way to make a copy of the document for your records. This can be a problem if you later need to verify your agreement's details or refer to correspondence during the disputing process. Should the dispute escalate to the point that a lawsuit is necessary, it can be difficult to prepare all the required documents for your attorney if you have exclusively communicated through the bureau's website.

A more significant complication to submitting online is that you waive away certain rights that you otherwise would have retained if you had sent it by air mail . Namely, you have a limited window of time to access the information relevant to the dispute. Once the dispute is resolved, even if it is not in your favor and you still want to pursue a dispute in court, you will have trouble accessing the online documents. If instead, you receive a paper copy of all relevant materials, you can keep these copies around for as long as you like without issue. Sometimes, you will not even be able to pursue a lawsuit with a jury involved if you decide to take the matter online. Before you can access the dispute, you'll be confronted with pop-up prompts that commonly have waivers of your rights as a consumer, including the right to sue. You won't be able to pursue a dispute without agreeing to these stipulations, putting you in a worse position than if you had just sent your dispute via mail.

Though it may seem slow and inconvenient if you grew up in the digital era, physical mail is a must when filing a credit dispute. It will save you a great deal of trouble in the future and you won't have to give up your right to litigate the matter if the bureau's investigation doesn't remove the offending item from your report. Remember, it's best to break out the pen and paper so you can write out your dispute.

**Batching Your Disputes**

When reviewing your credit report for inaccuracies, you may notice that you have more than one error. Grouping your disputes helps you avoid doing more busywork that drags out the dispute process. Still, not every dispute may belong in the same letter.

If you have multiple errors on a credit report from a single bureau, you can send a single letter. Just be sure to list the necessary account information for each incorrect item on the account. Suppose you have an error on multiple different credit reports. In that case, however, you cannot compile them all into a single letter, even if it is the exact error repeated across all three credit bureaus. Instead, you must make a separate dispute letter for each bureau. You can use the same template and wording as long as you send out individual letters for each bureau.

**Information to Include in a Dispute**

As mentioned in Chapter 4, a dispute letter must contain all of the information necessary for the bureau to locate your account and investigate the item in question. This includes basic identifying information about yourself. Make sure to write down your name, date of birth, social security number, and your current address, as well as any previous addresses you held in the last two years if they are different from your current home. You may also need to send in a photocopy of a government-issued ID and a utility bill or bank statement with your address on it for verification purposes.

Next, make a list of any inaccuracies on your credit report. Include the lender who holds or held the account, the account number, and the reasons why you believe the information is false. If you need to include any documents to prove this, make sure you send copies, not original documents, as the originals could get lost in the shuffle. Enclose your letter and the necessary documents in an envelope and write down the mailing address of the bureau. You're now ready to send the dispute notification and await the results of the bureau's investigation, at least theoretically. In practice, you will still want to optimize your dispute letters to make it through the OCR and e-OSCAR systems.

## UNDERSTANDING THE E-OSCAR SYSTEM

After spending time reviewing your credit report and writing out the proper letters, the last thing you want is for your dispute to be rejected or ignored with limited or no attention from an actual human. However, with the OCR and e-OSCAR systems, this is a distinct possibility. These systems are meant to sort the junk disputes from the ones that warrant investigating, but frequently they lead to the wrong categorization of the dispute letters from people who aren't well-versed in writing them.

The e-OSCAR system allows lenders and debt collectors to respond to requests for verification from a dispute automatically. Your dispute is reduced to a short code that indicates the type of dispute. While this shorthand is handy for allowing bureaus and creditors to process many disputes in a brief amount of time, it causes problems for the consumer. A potentially complex problem with supporting documentation gets oversimplified into a code and a brief description that may or may not include your submitted proof. Without proof, errors may be unclear, and your dispute is much more likely to be rejected.

### How to Fight Off E-OSCAR and Remove Derogatory Marks

If your dispute is rejected when you know it is valid, there's a good chance it didn't make it past the e-OSCAR system. Many people give up at this point, assuming there's nothing else they can do if they don't want to take the issue to court, but you still have options available to you. Start by requesting information about the method of verification from the credit bureau. Within 15 days, you should receive a response about the techniques used to verify the disputed information. You want to know that the bureau actually investigated your claim and that it did not simply make the rounds in the e-OSCAR system before getting verified automatically.

Remember that thanks to the FCRA, the laws are on your side. You have the right to demand an investigation when you file a dispute, and an e-OSCAR verification is not sufficient if no one reviewed the proof you sent. Ideally, you will get a response within 15 days, which involves the credit bureau reopening the investigation. Alternatively, you will have to take action. You can lodge a complaint with the Consumer Financial Protection Bureau, pointing out that the credit bureau did not comply with your request for a method of verification. In addition, you can file similar complaints with the Better Business Bureau and the state Attorney General. If all else fails, you can threaten the bureau with legal action if they still do not comply, though ideally, you shouldn't have to go to such extreme lengths to have the incorrect information removed from your credit report. Either way, if the item you're disputing is genuinely incorrect, it will eventually be taken off your credit report.

## ACHIEVE CREDIT EXCELLENCE

Credit repair isn't just about submitting disputes and hoping they turn out in your favor. In the big-picture view, repairing your credit is just one step on the path to credit excellence. You are submitting disputes for the sake of your credit score, which you want to raise to get favorable loans and lines of credit in the future. A healthy credit score is invaluable and it is well worth the work you put into credit repair when you scan your report and create dispute letters.

Always remember to point out the reasoning behind your disputes in your letters. Target all inaccuracies so bureaus can quickly remove them from your profile and they will no longer be able to harm your score. As you work through the dispute process, combine it with sustainable credit usage and other pointers discussed in this book thus far.

Focus on improving your credit score from the ground up, targeting other critical areas like having a decent credit mix, keeping up with monthly payments, and limiting how often you apply for new lines of credit. If you have trouble qualifying for credit, try a secured credit card or a credit-builder loan, both geared toward people looking to build their credit score. Keep track of all changes in your score and keep your credit utilization low each month to bring your score up even further. Create a budget, and if you need additional pointers, utilize nonprofit credit counseling services. Keep monitoring your score and credit reports for any strange activity that could indicate you need to file another dispute. With some hard work and the right motivation, your efforts will pay off, and you will be able to raise your credit all the way up to an excellent level.

## Sample Letters

If you're not exactly sure where to start, it's a good idea to reference a few sample dispute letters. These can help point you in the right direction when you write your own. One word of caution is to avoid relying too heavily on templates. The automated system always picks up these templates, and they can decrease your chances of having your dispute investigated appropriately. Put things in your own words, especially when explaining why you are disputing a given item. Additionally, always handwrite your letters rather than typing them up or filling out an online template.

You can find official sample letters online from government agencies, including the FTC and Treasury Department. Feel free to reference these or write a letter similar to this sample:

---

[Date]

[Your name]

[Address]

[Credit bureau business name]

[Address of the bureau]

Subject: Credit Report Dispute

I am writing to dispute incorrect information on my credit report that was supplied by [name of lender]. I have attached a copy of my credit report with the items I am disputing circled.

I am disputing the [type of item] from my account [account number] with [lender]. I believe this information is inaccurate because [reason for disputing the information]. I have attached [document] as proof of the inaccuracy. I am requesting that the item be [removed or corrected].

I am also disputing [type of item] from my account [account number] with [lender]. This information is inaccurate because [reason for the dispute]. I have attached [document] as proof of the inaccuracy, and I request that the item be [removed or corrected].

[Add additional disputed items if necessary]

Enclosed are [list of all documents] supporting my dispute. Please investigate the issue and make the necessary corrections as soon as possible.

Sincerely,

[Name]

---

## IDENTITY THEFT

If you are writing to remove information from your credit report resulting from identity theft, you will want to change your wording to indicate this. Identity theft is a serious crime and you will have to complete a few additional steps. First, it's best to file a police report. This notifies local police to be on the lookout for someone using your ID, but who doesn't look like you. Many creditors will require proof that you have filed a police report before they will take action on fraudulent claims, so it's best to complete this step right away. Next, contact all lenders where you have credit cards, as well as your bank. Close any accounts that were involved in the fraudulent activity. Open new accounts, ideally with additional protection to prevent the fraud from happening again.

Next, let the credit bureaus know you have been the victim of fraud so they can place a fraud alert on your accounts. This will prevent the thief from opening up any more new accounts in your name, meaning you'll have less to worry about when you dispute trade lines. You'll also want to file a report with the FTC and with the relevant creditors so they know the accounts were created or used without your knowledge. If a collection agency contacts you, let them know that the debt is not yours and that you will be disputing it, and that they no longer need to contact you about it.

When writing your letter to the credit bureaus to dispute the charges, you can use a structure similar to this sample:

[Date]

[Your name]

[Address]

[Credit bureau business name]

[Address of the bureau]

Subject: Identity Theft Dispute

I am writing to dispute incorrect information on my credit report that was the result of identity theft. I have attached a copy of my credit report with the fraudulent items I am disputing circled so they can be removed from my report.

I am disputing the [type of item] from my account [account number] with [lender]. I believe this information is inaccurate because [reason for disputing the information]. I have attached [document, typically a police report] as proof of the inaccuracy. I am requesting that the item be [removed].

[Add additional disputed items if necessary]

Enclosed are [list of all documents] supporting my dispute. Please investigate the issue and make the necessary corrections as soon as possible.

Sincerely,

[Name]

---

Whether you are disputing items related to identity fraud or information caused by a simple clerical error, dispute letters allow you to correct misinformation while boosting your score. However, even credit repair won't be enough to fix your debt and credit score situation in some cases. If the majority of the negative marks bringing down your score are legitimate, there is nothing to correct. If you have excessive levels of debt that cannot be managed by credit counseling and the debts cannot be settled, you may have to resort to more extreme measures. If all else fails, you can make a last-ditch effort to free yourself from debt by declaring bankruptcy.

# 8

# THE LAST RESORT

*"If we don't change, millions of American families are just one medical emergency, or one layoff, away from financial disaster and bankruptcy."*

— JIM COOPER

You've reviewed your credit report and disputed any inaccuracies. You've attempted to settle your debts to no avail, either because you owe too much money or because you don't have the savings to make a settlement payment. You've attended credit counseling, and you're unable to put most of the advice to good use because you don't have the money to save, stick to a budget, and pay down your debts. At this point, it can seem like you're backed into a corner with no options, but you still have a few. You could continue going the way you have been, gradually burning through your savings and dropping your credit score lower and lower, always trying to get out from under significant piles of debt, or you could file for bankruptcy.

Although it's often perceived as the easy way out, filing for bankruptcy isn't for the faint of heart. It has severe and long-lasting repercussions on your credit. It can make it significantly harder to qualify for credit in the future. Even after filing for bankruptcy, you may still be stuck paying off certain lines of credit that weren't wiped from your record. Still, it may be the right move in certain circumstances, mainly when you are in such a tight spot that you don't have any other options. Bankruptcy should only be used as a last resort, but there are some situations where it can benefit your credit in the long term, so long as you are willing to take the hit to your score in the short term.

## THE FOUR STEPS OF FILING FOR BANKRUPTCY

Many different types of bankruptcy serve different purposes. Some are better suited for businesses or individuals, while others help alleviate certain kinds of debt. No matter what type of bankruptcy you file, you will be granted an automatic stay on your current accounts as soon as you begin moving forward with the process. This means you will get immediate relief from creditors attempting to contact you for your outstanding debts. You will also be protected from having your wages garnished to pay off what you owe for a brief time. The automatic stay is meant to help you reorient yourself and better prepare you to resume payments on any debts that are not wiped out by bankruptcy.

Note that, while different kinds of bankruptcies target various sources of debt, there are some types of loans and credit lines that bankruptcy does not impact. These include child support, alimony, student loans, and tax debts, all of which are considered non-dischargeable. In other words, you will still be on the hook for paying them, so if you're looking to file for bankruptcy because you can't keep up with your student loan payments, you will have to look elsewhere.

The exact procedures involved in filling out and filing bankruptcy forms differ depending on the type of bankruptcy being declared. However, the general steps remain the same. They include attending credit counseling and other post-bankruptcy meetings, submitting the proper paperwork, and covering the filing fee.

**Step One: Pre-Bankruptcy Credit Counseling**

When you file for bankruptcy, you will be obligated to take a mandatory credit counseling course. This is meant to prevent you from having to file for bankruptcy again in the future. It is also mandated in the hopes of preventing people from unnecessarily jumping right to bankruptcy to fix their credit, as many people need just less extreme measures like improving their spending habits and developing a budget. You must complete credit counseling before submitting your bankruptcy paperwork and you must utilize credit counseling services that the government has approved. You can find a sortable database of all approved credit counselors on the U.S. Department of Justice website at justice.gov.

Credit counselors will work with you to determine whether or not an option other than bankruptcy might be right for you. Bankruptcy shouldn't be anyone's first choice, but many people don't know that there are other options available, so they end up unnecessarily hurting their credit score. Your counselor will walk you through all your options while also providing you with helpful tips for better managing your money and raising your credit score after taking the credit hit that comes with bankruptcy. Be sure to put the tips you learn during counseling into practice, even if you still want to go through with filing for bankruptcy. Turn these good practices into habits, so they become second nature. This will set you up to gradually repair your credit after bankruptcy.

When you complete the mandatory credit counseling, you will receive a valid certificate of completion for the next 180 days. You must file for bankruptcy within this timeframe or risk having to take credit counseling once again. Note that, after you have filed your paperwork, you will also be required to complete the pre-discharge debtor education program. In most cases, you can use the same company for credit counseling and debtor education, though you must complete each separately.

**Step Two: Filling Out Bankruptcy Forms**

Like many other government services, filing for bankruptcy involves filling out the appropriate forms and submitting them through the proper channels. If you're uncertain about the process and you want to make sure you do things right, you can hire an attorney to walk you through the entire process and take care of the submission for you. However, attorneys can be expensive and if you're staring bankruptcy in the face, you may not have the money to pay a professional. Luckily, you can complete these forms yourself as long as you read them carefully and fill them out entirely according to the directions on the paperwork.

Note that the kinds of information you'll need to provide for different types of bankruptcy differ from each other. Pay attention to what chapter you are filing under, as this will help you fill out the forms with the greatest accuracy. Even if you know what you're doing, this isn't a speedy process, so set aside some time to complete these forms. The questions on these forms will involve reporting your income, expenses, outstanding debts, and assets. Ensure you have all necessary information available when you fill out the forms so you don't have to hunt them down later.

**Step Three: Pay Your Filing Fee**

Filing for bankruptcy isn't free. The chapter you're filing under determines the fees. Fees vary from $100 to $600, though it is typically far cheaper for an individual to go bankrupt than for a company. Be sure to look up the exact fee for your filing method. If you already have the money in your savings, you'll be asked to pay it when you file your petition for bankruptcy with the court.

If you can't afford the filing fee, you have a few options available. The first is to save up for a few weeks or months until you have the requisite funds. Suppose you have already stopped paying your debts in preparation for bankruptcy. In that case, it may be easier for you to put a more significant chunk of your paycheck toward your savings so that you can come up with the money relatively quickly without issue. If this isn't a possibility for you, consider submitting an application and paying the fee in four monthly installments rather than one lump sum. These smaller installments are less draining on your budget, making them far more manageable for many people. Finally, if all else fails, you can try applying for a waiver. To qualify for a waiver, you will need to have a meager income that falls at least 150 percent below the poverty line, so this isn't a feasible option for most people. It's best to start saving up before you begin pursuing bankruptcy so that you can pull together the adequate funds.

Once you have your fee and all of your forms, it's time to submit them. Print your forms on single-sided paper, sign them where indicated, and collect other relevant documents, including your certificate from credit counseling, your paycheck stubs to prove your income, and any additional paperwork mandated by your state. Depending on your state's laws, you may need to make multiple copies of all your documents, including the bankruptcy forms.

Finally, head to your nearest courthouse and let the clerk know you are filing for bankruptcy. After the clerk has scanned all your forms, they will provide you with a case number and contact information for your bankruptcy trustee, who will oversee the process moving forward.

### Step Four: Attend the Necessary Post-Bankruptcy Meetings and Courses

Even after submitting the proper forms, you're not entirely free and in the clear just yet. Instead, you are still required to attend two important meetings. The first is the aforementioned debtor education course. Note that typically you can take this course online or over the phone rather than having to schedule an in-person visit. Most classes take two to three hours and require a fee, typically around $50. Once you've completed the course, file your certificate with the court to include it on your record.

You will also have to attend a meeting of creditors, also known as a 341 meeting. This is a very brief meeting, usually held over the phone, involving verifying some basic information. Keep your ID and social security card close by, as well as any documents requested by your trustee. These can include pay stubs, a copy of your bankruptcy paperwork, and other documents used as proof of your identity. You'll be automatically assigned a time and date for your 341 meeting on your court notice when you file for bankruptcy.

## BANKRUPTCY TYPES

When you're considering whether or not bankruptcy is the right move for you, make sure to also give some thought to which type of bankruptcy best suits your current situation. There are six different kinds of bankruptcies, known as chapters, and they are all used for distinct purposes. Some are meant for individuals or businesses, while others are used for certain kinds of occupations and companies. Luckily, you don't have to memorize all six bankruptcy chapters. You can focus on those that are most likely to be relevant to your situation. For most individual filers, you only need to worry about Chapter 7, Chapter 11, and Chapter 13.

### **Chapter** 7

Chapter 7 bankruptcy is also known as liquidation. It is used by most individuals filing for bankruptcy partly because it is the most straightforward method. All of your available assets are liquidated and the resulting funds are used to pay off your debts. Whatever remains is then erased, aside from those debts that are not affected by bankruptcy. Liquidation provides one of the quickest paths to debt relief, but keep in mind that you may be forced to relinquish any valuable items in your possession. Typically, you will be allowed to keep significant assets like your home and car, as well as the funds in your retirement account. You only need to agree to continue paying any debts on these properties through a process known as reaffirming your loans. You may, however, lose high-value property that is not considered exempt.

If you have nothing to sell that qualifies for liquidation, you can still proceed with a Chapter 7. Your trustee will file your bankruptcy as a "no asset" report instead. This means the creditors don't get paid, but your debts will still be waived. Most people filing Chapter 7 bankruptcy don't have any eligible assets. Still, you will be forced to turn them over if you do, so keep this in mind before deciding to continue pursuing bankruptcy.

Chapter 7 bankruptcy is only available if you do not have the means to pay your debts back. The court will examine your savings and income and determine whether or not you are granted bankruptcy. Chapter 7 is best suited for people with low incomes, though keep in mind that it comes with the added commitment of having the bankruptcy on your account for ten years. You also cannot file for bankruptcy again for eight years, so be sure to make the most of your fresh start.

**Chapter 11**

Chapter 11 bankruptcy is used for large organizations. Usually applying to businesses, it allows them to continue operating while still formulating a plan for paying off or settling their existing debts. It is a little less common than Chapters 7 and 13, but it may be relevant for you if you invest in real estate or have other valuable assets that would disqualify you for Chapter 7 bankruptcy.

Since Chapter 11 bankruptcy involves higher-value properties, the filing fee is higher as well. You can expect to pay upwards of $1,000, and you will still be expected to reach an agreement with your creditors and the court about a repayment process. Still, it is far less costly than simply selling your valuable assets, making Chapter 11 a viable alternative for small business owners who have fallen on hard times.

**Chapter 13**

Chapter 13 bankruptcy is known as a repayment plan. Rather than forgiving all of your debt that you cannot pay from the sale of assets, a Chapter 13 bankruptcy provides you with an opportunity to reorganize it into a regular payment plan. The court will assist you in establishing a set of objectives that take into consideration your limited resources while still paying creditors enough that they are willing to accept a settlement. You will have to pay back all of your secured debt, but only a tiny portion of your unsecured debt, so you typically end up paying less than you would with a standard debt settlement program. You also get to keep your assets, though you do have to abide by a court-mandated budget and surveillance of your spending habits.

Note that if you file for Chapter 13 bankruptcy, but fail to hold up your end of the bargain by sticking to your payment plan, there will be serious consequences. Objectives are designed to be manageable for your financial situation, so avoid taking out any additional debts or paying for expensive items that might make it more difficult for you to keep up with your payments. Otherwise, you could find yourself back in court.

Chapter 13 bankruptcies remain on your record for seven years, and you will have to wait at least two years before filing for bankruptcy again. You will only qualify for this type of bankruptcy if you have less than $419,275 in unsecured debt and less than $1,257,850 in secured debt, though this should be well within reason for most individual filers.

## YOUR FRESH START

Bankruptcy isn't an ideal way to deal with your debt, but that doesn't mean that it's all bad. If you are backed into a corner with no other options, there are plenty of things to appreciate about the period after you file for bankruptcy. First, and most significantly, your debt is significantly reduced if not eliminated entirely. A few kinds of debt aren't erased, but in general, the vast majority of them will either be waived or repaid on a plan that is exceedingly more manageable than before. This alleviation of debt is a huge relief, as you will no longer have to spend so much time and energy stressing about how you're going to pay off what you owe. You can live without the fear of your wages being garnished or being sued, and you will no longer be dodging calls from angry creditors and collection agencies. This makes a significant difference in reducing your levels of debt-related worry and anxiety, and it can do wonders for your mood.

The alleviation of past debts also means you get to enjoy, more or less, a fresh start when it comes to credit and money habits. You have an opportunity to start over and handle things the right way this time; don't rack up so much debt in the future. Put the skills you've learned in credit counseling to good use. Start by building up an emergency fund in your savings so you're prepared for any unexpected incidents that would otherwise drain your bank account. Make an effort to borrow only as much as you can afford to pay off in full each month whenever possible. Downsize in various areas of your life by making small changes like going out to eat less often or clipping coupons when you go shopping. Put good money habits into practice now to prevent yourself from going into such significant debt again in the future. Going through the bankruptcy process is tough, but if you view it as an opportunity for improvement, you can make the best of a bad situation.

**Looking on The Bright Side**

Many people have concerns about their ability to repair their credit score once they've decided to pursue bankruptcy. These concerns aren't unfounded. Bankruptcy does lower your credit score, and the effect remains for seven to ten years, depending on the type of bankruptcy. However, this doesn't mean you will be stuck with poor credit forever. The vast majority of people actually find that the opposite is true, and after some time, their scores begin to rise.

Credit score improvement is due to several factors. For one, if you're in a position where you're considering bankruptcy, you probably already have a low score. You've likely missed payments on your debts multiple times and there's no way for you to pay them off without continuing this spotty track record. You might have numerous charge-offs and repossessions and there's a good chance you've had more than a few debts fall into collections. Altogether, these problems caused your credit score to take a big hit. But once you no longer have any delinquent debts due to filing for bankruptcy, you may find that your credit score rebounds reasonably quickly, despite the bankruptcy penalty.

In a study of Equifax credit reports, Federal Reserve researchers in Philadelphia found that credit scores took a nosedive in the 18 months prior to filing and steadily rose thereafter. This isn't to say everything is smooth sailing, as you'll likely find it much more challenging to get approved for loans and new lines of credit for a few years, but with patience and careful money management, you can and will restore your credit.

Be sure to use the methods previously covered in this book, such as credit counseling and credit repair, to your advantage. If you practice good spending habits and you're serious about wanting to improve your credit, it's not unreasonable to expect to achieve a fair or reliable credit score within a year of filing for bankruptcy. Remember that your credit score is never set in stone. No matter how bad things get, whether you decide to file for bankruptcy or not, you can always take steps to improve your credit, and your efforts will be rewarded with better rates and less financial stress.

# CONCLUSION

Poor credit is a common problem for millions of Americans, but it doesn't have to be permanent. You have many options available to you when you're ready to get serious about taking back control of your finances, all of which you have learned about while reading this book:

- You can meet with a credit counselor to get a personal review of your financial situation and employ the best methods for staying on top of your debts and raising your credit over time.
- You can use debt settlement to significantly reduce the amount you owe, allowing you to become debt-free much faster.
- You can review your credit report for potential

errors that could be lowering your score without your knowledge.
- You can even file for bankruptcy if there's no other way to alleviate issues with debt.

Each option has its pros and cons, and each is best suited to different situations. Consider which method(s) seem effective for dealing with your most significant financial troubles and feel free to combine methods as you work to raise your score.

Repairing your credit can take anywhere from a few months to a few years, so don't give up hope if you don't see change right away. Develop a plan of attack and stick to it or enlist the help of credit counselors to point you in the right direction. You now know everything you need to fix your credit, no matter how good or bad it may be. All that's left is to put these skills into practice, raise your score, and enjoy the benefits of financial peace of mind.

If you found this a valuable book on your credit restoration journey, please be sure to leave an honest review on Amazon. This lets other people struggling with debt know that there's a way out, so they too can learn how to repair their credit and enjoy newfound financial freedom.

## DON'T FORGET TO GET THE MOST OUT OF THIS BOOK

If you're genuinely curious, willing to make changes, and take action, you can be on your way towards a debt-free future. To help you on your journey, I have created a free workbook that includes an easy to use budgeting sheet & debt calculator to determine your debt-free date. Use this tool to guide you in accomplishing your goals.

To get the most out of this book, sign up now by visiting the link below:

https://allenanything.com

SCAN ME

# REFERENCES

Androitis, A. (2013, Aug. 8). *10 things credit bureaus won't say*. MarketWatch. https://www.marketwatch.com/story/10-things-credit-bureaus-wont-say-2013-02-15

Board of Governors of the Federal Reserve System. (2018, May 22). *Federal Reserve board issues report on economic well-being of U.S. households.* Federal Reserve. https://www.federalreserve.gov/newsevents/pressreleases/other20180522a.htm

CFPB Consumer Laws and Regulations. (2012, Oct.). *Fair credit reporting act*. Consumer Financial Protection Bureau. https://files.consumerfinance.gov/f/documents/102012_cfpb_fair-credit-reporting-act-fcra_procedures.pdf

Consumer Financial Protection Bureau. (2018, Feb 2). *What is credit counseling?* https://www.consumerfinance.gov/ask-cfpb/what-is-credit-counseling-en-1451/

Depersio, G. (2021, May 3). *FICO vs. Experian vs. Equifax: What's the difference?* Investopedia. https://www.investopedia.com/articles/credit-loans-mortgages/082816/fico-vs-experian-vs-equifax-their-pros-and-cons-fico-efx.asp

Egan, J. & Strohm, M. (2021, Jun 10). *Debt settlement: How it works and is it worth the risk?* Forbes Advisor. https://www.forbes.com/advisor/debt-relief/debt-settlement-how-it-works-and-risks/

Eneriz, A. (2021, Apr. 8). *This easy trick will improve your credit score and avoid late payments.* Go Banking Rates. https://www.gobankingrates.com/credit/credit-score/easy-trick-improve-credit-score-avoid-late-payments/

Experian. (n.d.-a). *What is a credit utilization rate?* https://www.experian.com/blogs/ask-experian/credit-education/score-basics/credit-utilization-rate/

Experian. (n.d.-b). *Understanding the fair credit reporting act.* https://www.experian.com/blogs/ask-experian/credit-education/report-basics/fair-credit-reporting-act-fcra/

Fay, M. (n.d.). *Credit counseling vs. bankruptcy*. Debt.org. https://www.debt.org/bankruptcy/vs-credit-counseling/

Fontinelle, A. (2021, June 16). *Debt settlement: Cheapest way to get out of debt?* Investopedia. https://www.investopedia.com/personal-finance/debt-settlement-cheapest-way-get-out-debt/

Jackson, T. (n.d.). *Credit repair vs. credit counseling*. InCharge. https://www.incharge.org/debt-relief/credit-counseling/credit-repair-vs-credit-counseling/

Lyngklip & Associates. (n.d.). *Should I make my credit dispute online?* Consumer Lawyers. https://www.consumerlawyers.com/should-i-make-my-credit-dispute-over-the-web

McClary, B. (2020, May 12). *The short and long-term effects of debt settlement: What consumers can expect through the process and how long it may take to rebound*. National Foundation for Credit Counseling. https://www.nfcc.org/resources/blog/the-short-and-long-term-effects-of-debt-settlement/

Pritchard, J. (2021, May 31). *How credit bureaus work*. The Balance. https://www.thebalance.com/how-credit-bureaus-work-315540

Ramsey, D. (2021, Sept. 13). *What are the different types of bankruptcies?* Ramsey Solutions. https://www.ramseysolutions.com/debt/types-of-bankruptcies

Ulzheimer, J. (2012, June 18). *Is credit repair right for me?* Intuit MintLife. https://mint.intuit.com/blog/credit/is-credit-repair-right-for-me-062012/

Ulzheimer, J. (2021, May 6). *The 609 dispute letter myth.* CreditVersio. https://www.creditversio.com/credit-coaching/blog?p=the-609-dispute-letter-myth

Weston, L. (2021, Aug. 6). *When bankruptcy is the best option.* Nerdwallet. https://www.nerdwallet.com/article/finance/bankruptcy-best-option

White, J. (2020, June 28). *What is the difference between credit counseling and debt settlement?* Experian. https://www.experian.com/blogs/ask-experian/the-difference-between-credit-counseling-and-debt-settlement-2/

Wimmer, A. (2020, Dec. 28). *How to file bankruptcy in 2021 for free: A 10-step guide.* Upsolve. https://upsolve.org/learn/how-to-file-bankruptcy

Made in United States
Troutdale, OR
11/03/2026

56847380R00104